PUB WALKS

IN

North Yorkshire

FORTY CIRCULAR WALKS
AROUND NORTH YORKSHIRE INNS

Leonard Markham

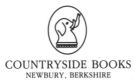

COUNTRYSIDE BOOKS
NEWBURY, BERKSHIRE

COUNTRYSIDE BOOKS
3 Catherine Road
Newbury, Berkshire

ISBN 1 85306 182 4

Publisher's Note

We hope that you obtain considerable enjoyment from this book; great care
has been taken in its preparation. However, changes of landlord and actual
closures are sadly not uncommon. Likewise, although at the time of
publication all routes followed public rights of way or well-established
permitted paths, diversion orders can be made and permissions withdrawn.

We cannot accept responsibility for any inaccuracies, but we are anxious
that all details covering both pubs and walks are kept up to date, and would
therefore welcome information from readers which would be relevant to
future editions.

Photographs by the author
Maps by Ian Streets
Cover illustration by Colin Doggett

Produced through MRM Associates Ltd., Reading
Typeset by Paragon Typesetters, Sandycroft, Chester
Printed in England

For Christine
(the indefatigable)

Contents

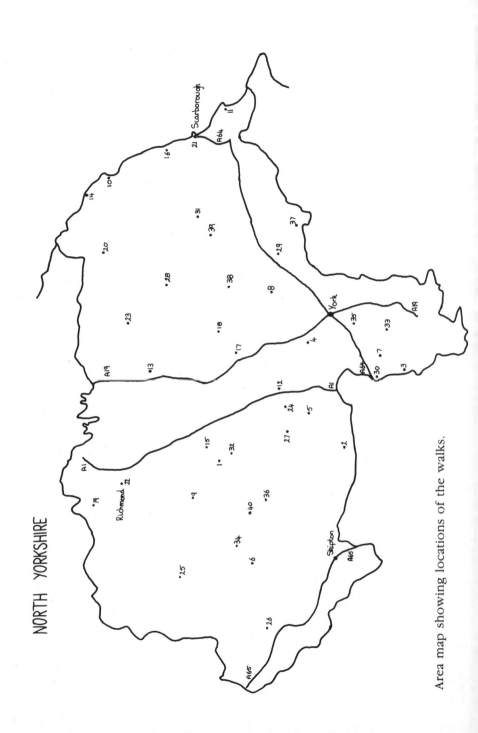

NORTH YORKSHIRE

Area map showing locations of the walks.

Introduction

Have you memories of cherished paths and byways? Do you recall that cool cascade, those purpled moors, that painted swinging board? And do your recollections turn to thoughts of that favourite inn, remembering the relish that honest toil imparted to your Yorkshire pudding and onion gravy?

If, like me, you prize these precious slices of England, then I hope that this book will encourage you to explore again, for there is no finer county in which to sharpen one's appetite than North Yorkshire.

The sketch map which accompanies each walk is designed to give a simple yet accurate idea of the route to be taken. For those who like a more detailed map, the relevant number in the OS Landranger 1:50 000 series (or the Outdoor Leisure series) is also given. Please remember the Country Code and make sure gates are not left open or any farm animals disturbed.

No special equipment is needed to enjoy the countryside on foot, but do wear a stout pair of shoes and remember that at least one muddy patch is likely even on the sunniest day. Do please also remember that even the most accommodating of inn landlords is unlikely to welcome walkers with muddy boots, and leave yours outside the pub when you return.

Many of the walks in this book recommend leaving your car in the inn car park, with the intention of eating or drinking at the inn on your return. If you do so, particularly outside normal opening hours, please ask the landlord's permission. A car left for hours in an otherwise empty car park may become an object of suspicion.

There are 40 good walks and 40 good pubs within these pages. I have chosen mostly short, easy gradient routes so that even those of average fitness need have no fear of fatigue. To suit your moods, and the weather, I have included a variety of walks, treading the magnificent Yorkshire coast in the east, the quiet pastoral dales mid-county and the wild bog country in the west. A dyed-in-the-wool Tyke not given to exaggeration, I can vouch that all the walks offer clean fresh air in abundance, the friendliest of confrontations with nature, a modicum of historical and architectural interest, and the most pleasurable method of raising a thirst yet known to man.

Leonard Markham
Barwick-in-Elmet

Masham
The King's Head

A soothing distance from through traffic, this former coaching inn and excise house stands in a broad market square, the spacious venue for Masham's colourful September sheep fair. Owned by local brewers Theakston, the King's Head successfully blends liveliness and relaxation, having developed a dependable reputation for fine food and ale.

Offering ten en-suite bedrooms with full facilities, the inn is a popular tourist base for exploring the eastern dales. Also catering for day visitors and the local business and farming community, the King's Head provides an extensive range of both informal and formal meals. Served in the light and airy public bar the standard bar menu includes grilled local trout, home-made steak and kidney pie and Old Peculier casserole (Old Peculier is a sweet, resinous, strong ale unique to Theakston) complemented by daily blackboard specials. Dark oak provides the contrasting intimacy for diners in the 55 cover restaurant where the local brew is again put to culinary use, this time through deep fried mushrooms in beer batter. Developing the indigenous theme, Wensleydale soufflé uses the excellent local cheese. Amongst the range of other starters, grilled scallops in a lemon and chive butter with a Gruyere cheese gratin is particularly noteworthy. Main courses feature rack of Yorkshire lamb stuffed with minced mushrooms and onions, grilled bacon-wrapped fillet steak filled with Stilton cheese, breast of duck, escalope of salmon and baked trout. Three distinctive hand-pulled beers complement the food — Theakston Bitter, Old Peculier and XB. Of the same pedigree, a recent introduction is the strong Masham Ale in bottle. Harp and Becks lagers, and draught Guinness and Strongbow cider complete the line-up.

The inn is open Monday to Saturday 11 am to 11 pm and Sunday 12 noon to 3 pm and 7 pm to 10.30 pm. The restaurant is open between 7 pm and 9.30 pm daily.

Telephone: 0765-689295.

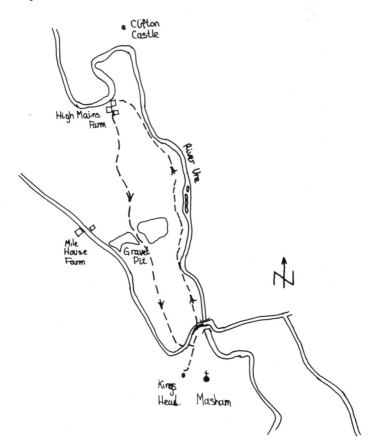

How to get there: The inn is in Masham's extensive Market Place.

Parking: Park in the Market Place.

Length of the walk: 4 miles. OS Map Landranger series No. 99 (inn GR 223808).

A pleasant amble along the wooded banks of the Ure, on the return journey disturbing the gravel pit roosts of black headed gulls and oyster-catchers.

The Walk
Walk to the A6108 Ure Bridge, with the old North of England Malt Roasting Company warehouse to your left. Turn left on the riverside path and follow it over a series of stiles and footbridges upstream for 1¼ miles to a fenced wood (Swinton Estate – No Access) and a small island where the river divides when in flood. Turn left uphill and follow the river course on a bank-top path. Clifton Castle (built 1810) comes into view on the river's left bank.

Swing left behind and through High Mains Farm and continue on a farm track past Low Mains Farm. Ignoring the 90° road access to the right, continue on through a meadow, passing between two gravel pits readily colonised by flocks of sea birds. Pass through Redland Aggregates entrance by the gatehouse. Turn right uphill for 20 yards and then turn left through a field aiming diagonally right for a distant steeple. Take the track between two hedges back into Masham.

Other local attractions: Theakston Brewery visitor centre and brewery tours, Uredale Glassworks (rear of King's Head) and St. Mary's church.

North Rigton
The Square and Compass

On a pastoral canvas, the inspiration for a succession of distinguished artists, the lofty Square and Compass and its village look out onto Wharfedale. One of the two principal trysting places in North Rigton (the nearby crag of Alms Cliff attracts an equal number of visitors), this immensely spacious hostelry offers hospitality in abundance.

Dating from 1274, the once thatched building, which was a rendezvous for the Wharfedale otter hounds in the 1930s, has since been extended to provide an airy lounge, luxuriously appointed in red velvet, a pool room, an intimate cocktail lounge, and a large 100 seater restaurant/function facility, all tastefully decorated with prints, a mixture of old and modern photographs and pot plants. The inn offers a lavish range of bar snacks and a more formal menu for evening and weekend diners. The varied bar snacks menu includes a de luxe range of sandwiches such as smoked salmon on rye bread, steak and kidney pie, roast chicken and salmon in white wine. The 40-seater restaurant offers such specialities as broccoli and Stilton quiche, sole and trout terrine, contrafillet of beef with smoked bacon, chicken and mushroom vol-au-vents and trout fillet with almonds. Children are

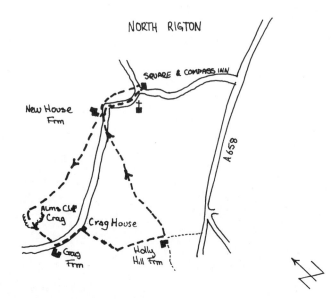

welcome in the restaurant, which is open on Thursday, Friday and Saturday evenings. The house ales are hand-pulled Younger Scotch and No. 3 bitter supported by McEwan and Becks lagers, draught Guinness and Bulmers cider.

Opening times are from 11.30 am to 2.30 pm and 5.30 pm to 11 pm Monday to Saturday and 12 noon to 3 pm and 7.30 pm to 10.30 pm on Sundays.

Telephone: 0423-734228.

How to get there: The inn stands in an elevated position in the landmark village of North Rigton, off the main A658 Pool to Harrogate road.

Parking: Park in the inn car park.

Length of the walk: 2½ miles. OS Map Landranger series No. 104 (inn GR 281493).

An invigorating horizon's walk over green fields, visiting Alms Cliff crag. Relish the best of Wharfedale's scenery and hark to the curlew nocturnes, rising like bubbles on the wind.

12

The Walk

Turn right past the village stocks on the road signposted to Huby, to St. John's church on the left. A brief visit will reward you with exquisite views and a chance to find, on the oaken communion rail, the famous 'cowering timorous beastie' trademark of Thompsons of Kilburn. Continue to the junction with the quiet Crag Lane and turn right uphill to greet the imposing eminence of Alms Cliff crag. Pass Newhouse Farm and take the marked footpath on the right to the crag summit. On a clear day the White Horse of Kilburn (the home of that mouse) rears on the eastern panorama.

Descend to the left, heading south in the direction of Crag Farm. Cross a stile, turn left along the road to Crag House and take the descending footpath, veering right in the meadow to a wrought iron stile. Turn left via a series of stiles to the edge of a coniferous plantation and proceed along a concreted track to Holly Hill Farm. Turn north and sharp left on a stiled steeplechase of brooks and thorn fences to rejoin the road. Turn right and, near New House Farm, take the marked footpath to North Rigton. Turn left and left again to return to the inn car park.

Other local attractions: Harewood House and Bird Garden.

The nearby Alms Cliff crag attracts climbers and visitors.

13

Saxton
The Crooked Billet

An attractive wayfarers inn standing alone on the windswept road to Tadcaster, the Crooked Billet offers a warm welcome and some of the biggest Yorkshire puddings in the county. With a farmhouse kitchen atmosphere, the homely interior, warmed by cheery brasses and log fires, comprises a cosy snug, an extended dining area, and a bar carved with the emblems of the feuding houses of York and Lancaster. The heraldry of Edward IV, the Yorkist champion of nearby Towton Moor, where in 1461 upwards of 30,000 men were killed in the bloodiest battle ever fought on English soil, is commemorated in the inn sign (crossed sticks, or in the local vernacular 't' creukt billets'). A booklet, available at the bar, tells the full story of the battle.

A John Smith's house, serving a tangy hand-pulled bitter, the inn's gastronomic theme is that of the giant Yorkshire pudding, royally appointed with a variety of cosmopolitan fillings including chilli and curry! Less Gulliverian diners are catered for in a selection of chicken and steak dishes, fresh sandwiches and home-made pot meals. Children are catered for until 8 pm.

Opening hours are from 11.30 am until 3 pm and 6.30 pm until

14

11 pm Monday to Saturday, and 12 noon until 3 pm and 7 pm until
10.30 pm on Sundays.
   Telephone: 0937-557389.

How to get there: The inn is on the B1217 between Towton and the
A1(T) at Hook Moor.

Parking: Park in the inn car park.

Length of the walk: 2½ miles. OS Map Landranger series No. 105
(inn GR 465366).

*This fascinating short amble, on the edge of the atmospheric Towton Moor,
discovers the sleepy village of Saxton, whose ancient cottages have the same
provenance as the stones of York Minster. Visit the tomb of Lord Dacre, who, with
his charger, was buried in Saxton churchyard after the battle of 1461, and, on the
banks of the Cock Beck, seek out the famous Towton rose whose petals are said to
be tinged with the blood of the fallen.*

The Walk
Leaving the car park in an easterly direction, walk on the field side of
the old orchard uphill to a gap in the hedge, where the tower of
Saxton church comes into view. Across fields, follow a line of pylons
and telegraph poles into Saxton, mounting a stile into what appears to

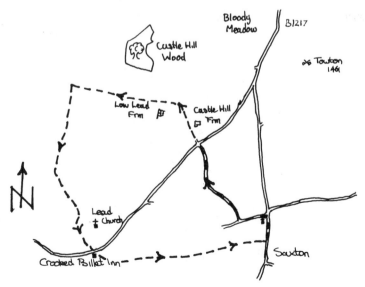

be a private garden (the owner confirms public right of access). At the road, turn left past the Greyhound Inn, and turn left again by the church.

Take the next right up a leafy lane to Castle Hill Cottage and cross the B1217 towards Castle Hill Farm. Cross the Cock Beck near Low Lead Farm, noticing the brooding Bloody Meadow on the skyline to the north. Continue on an ascending limestone track to a line of sycamore trees and turn left. On attaining the rise, the delightful chapel of St. Mary Lead comes into view.

Descend in the direction of Lead Hall Farm and proceed through a farm gate to a stile into the church meadow. Before recrossing the Cock Beck and returning to the Crooked Billet inn, take time to visit the little church.

Other local attractions: Lotherton Hall and Bird Garden and Scarthingwell Antiques Centre.

Nun Monkton
The Alice Hawthorn

4

Named after the famous winner of over 50 races, the inn is 'out to grass' on what is one of the largest village greens in England. Complemented by a maypole, a village pond and the encircling arms of the rivers Nidd and Ouse which have contrived a splendid isolation breached only by a single road, the Alice Hawthorn inn is well worth seeking out. Enthusiastically run, this war-time haunt of Canadian air crews from the nearby base at Linton-on-Ouse is homely and unpretentious, its simply furnished and relaxing bar nostalgically decorated with Bomber Command memorabilia.

The tranquil atmosphere pervades the large games/function room (the scene for early morning assemblies of anglers), the lounge and the dining room, where an extensive range of freshly cooked bar meals are on offer. Under starter's orders, peppered mackerel fillet and garlic mushrooms are well worth a flutter, the association with the turf being handsomely echoed in a main course presentation of hunter's casserole, a concoction of braised venison with wine, cream and port garnished with button mushrooms, onions and bacon. Other ample fare includes chicken breast filled with leeks and Stilton cheese, fillet of salmon, a range of prime steaks, and home-baked steak pie. Finely cellared hand-pulled Cameron Bitter, Tetley Bitter and Guinness, together with Castlemaine lager and Dry Blackthorn cider, complete the card. A small walled beer garden at the front of the inn allows you to sip and watch the cows graze by. Children are welcome.

The inn is open Monday to Saturday 12 noon to 2 pm and 7 pm to 11 pm and Sunday 12 noon to 3 pm and 7 pm to 10.30 pm.

Telephone: 0423-330303.

How to get there: The inn is in the village of Nun Monkton at the end of Pool Lane, off the A59 between York and Green Hammerton.

Parking: Park in the inn car park or beside the village green.

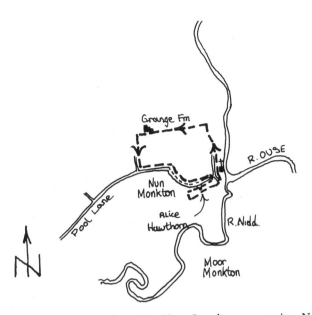

Length of the walk: 2½ miles. OS Map Landranger series No. 105 (inn GR 508578).

A leisurely amble around the Saxon village of Nun Monkton.

The Walk

Turning left from the inn, walk along the edge of the green and turn left past several cottages to a white gate. Go through and turn left by a second gate (note the Bradford No 1 Angling Club sign). Continue on the footpath at the rear of the village and turn left to a road. Turn right along a magnificent tree-lined avenue towards St. Mary's church and turn right by Nun Monkton Hall and left by a topiaried boundary to the confluence of the Nidd and Ouse. The valiant airmen crossed here for their well earned ale. Return journeys, I understand, were as dangerous as the Luftwaffe.

Return along the avenue to the Lodge (if a sign board is displayed at this house you are in luck. Mrs Susan Smith makes four varieties of delicious fudge. Try it). Back track once again and take the left-hand path over a decorative bridge onto a farm road. Proceed along this arcing road for 1½ miles to Pool Lane and turn left to return to the village.

Other local attractions: St. Mary's 12th century church and local trotting races in season.

19

Knaresborough
The Mother Shipton

Aptly named, within a wand's distance of the magical petrifying well and cave, the Mother Shipton is one of Knaresborough's more bewitching inns, attracting customers on the trail of the soothsayer whose predictions brought fame to the town.

Under the baleful gaze of the inn sign, visitors enter a welcoming and relaxing lounge enriched by wainscotting, original beams and a wealth of antiques. The diner may relax in a genuine Chippendale chair, eating from a table said to have belonged to Guy Fawkes. A burnished settle, a 17th century grandfather clock, rustic brasses and prints and an armoury of firearms over the mantelpiece add to the period feeling.

Judging by the home cooking, Old Mother Shipton is undeserving of her fearsome reputation, serving as she does gargantuan mixed grills and generous Barnsley chops, steaks, steak pies, scampi, plaice, haddock, hot and cold sandwiches and a selection of appetising starters and sweets. Liquid fare is no less nutritious, the dollopy Theakston Old Peculier and Guinness heading the calorific list, closely followed by beautifully kept, hand-pulled Younger Bitter and No. 3,

Theakston XB and Bitter, and Scrumpy Jack cider. Lager drinkers can opt for Becks' or McEwan's and wee-drammers may enjoy a geographical tour of the Highlands and Islands choosing one of 52 malts. An outstanding feature of the inn is the large well equipped beer garden next to the river Nidd.

There are many colourful traditions in Knaresborough and the Mother Shipton Inn has its own, performed on Boxing Day each year, snow or shine. Customers are asked to take the strain against rival drinkers from the Half Moon on the Nidd's far bank in an exciting tug of war. In all of the last 18 years, the Mother Shiptoners have endured a Christmas swim. Does this explain the large helpings?

The inn is open daily from 11.30 am to 3 pm and 5.30 pm to 11 pm Monday to Saturday and 12 noon to 3 pm and 7 pm to 10.30 pm Sunday. Occasional all day openings in heatwaves and at tugging time.

Telephone: 0423-862157.

How to get there: On the B6163, the inn is adjacent to Low Bridge spanning the Nidd.

Parking: Park in the small car park adjacent to the inn, use alternative free facilities across the bridge or, if intending to complete the full circuit through the Mother Shipton estate (fee payable), take advantage of inclusive parking facilities there.

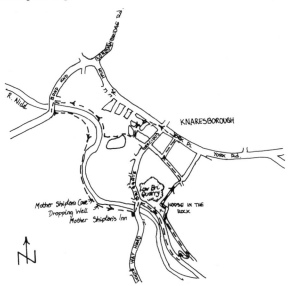

Length of the walk: 1½ miles. OS Map Landranger series No. 104 (inn GR 344571).

An exciting ramble of intrigue and eccentricity offering breathless views of the Nidd gorge. The route visits a peculiar troglodyte house, the oldest 'Chymist shoppe' in England, a royal castle and the cave where England's most famous prophetess was born. Gradient-drained, you may return to the inn by boat. Vessels may be hired nearby.

The Walk

From the inn, cross the bridge and turn right down Abbey Road, noticing the bizarre house in the rock (unable to secure a mortgage on a rock face, a local prospector set to with a pick; 14 years later he had his home and no financial worries). Continue past a sheer cliff and take a wriggling track on the left, ascending to Abbey Mount and a footpath sign marked 'Town Centre'. Turn left and enjoy long distance views of the ancient Forest of Knaresborough. Following the edge of Low Bridge quarry, proceed down Crag Lane and turn left again down Stockdale Walk and right along Iles Lane to York Place. Continue left over the junction, ignoring the attractions of the Board Inn and the Little Elephant on Silver Street, to Market Place and the chemist's shop of 1720.

Turn left via Castle Gate and right again to the castle precincts, where you may need ear protectors if you too encounter the town crier. After inspecting the castle take an avalanche of steps down to the river. At this stage you may wish to turn left to Low Bridge and return to the inn. Otherwise, turn right to High Bridge, cross the river and turn left to the Mother Shipton estate. Enter the grounds (fee payable) and proceed via the cave and the dropping well back to the inn.

Other local attractions: Free fishing in the Nidd, St. John the Baptist's church (Slingsby Chapel).

> Carriages without horses shall go,
> And accidents fill the world with woe.
> Around the world thoughts shall fly,
> In the twinkling of an eye.
> Iron in the water shall float,
> As easy as a wooden boat.
> Gold shall be found, and
> Found in a land that's not now known.

> Mother Shipton
> (16th century)

6 Litton
The Queen's Arms

In the heart of Littondale, the 'Queen of Yorkshire Dales', this sovereign little inn is a boon to walkers. At the spoke of intersecting long distance paths, the Queen's was described by a Victorian writer as 'a home from home in the heart of the hills', and it has hardly changed, stone flagged floors, mullioned windows and drunken timbers emphasising a reassuring permanence in this changeless landscape of hills and drystone walls.

Enjoy your hand-pulled Younger Scotch Bitter, McEwan lager or draught Guinness and gaze at the fells contesting half the sky, while choosing from varied lunchtime and evening menus. Home-made mid-day meals include steak and kidney pie with Guinness, chicken and mushroom pie, rabbit pie, broccoli and cheese bake and ploughman's lunch. Evening fare, which is also served in the pine-ceilinged best bar (ties are sometimes worn!), features garlic mushrooms, jeta cheese salad and queen's grill, fillet and sirloin steak, leek and mushroom bake, and peppers and mushrooms in a creamed sauce served in Yorkshire puddings. In the shooting season, pheasant, teal, grouse and venison dishes are available. Sweets range from lemon

tart and almond gateau to fresh raspberries. The Queen's has four
letting bedrooms, a field for campers and an attractive beer garden.
Children are welcome.

Opening hours are generally from Monday to Saturday from 11 am
to 3 pm and 7 pm to 11 pm, and Sunday from 12 noon to 3 pm and
7 pm to 10.30 pm, although in summer the taps are never draped on
Saturday and from the middle of July to early September the inn is
open all day, everyday.

Telephone: 0756 770208.

How to get there: The inn is in the village of Litton in the Yorkshire
Dales National Park near Kettlewell.

Parking: Park in front of the inn, or carefully (restricted width –
tractors coming!) on the roadside.

Length of the walk: 2¼ miles. OS Map Outdoor Leisure series No. 30
(inn GR 908741).

*This is a stroll by the Skirfare river, which flows underground along fissures in
the porous limestone rock, and a chance to investigate some of the geology of the
Dales.*

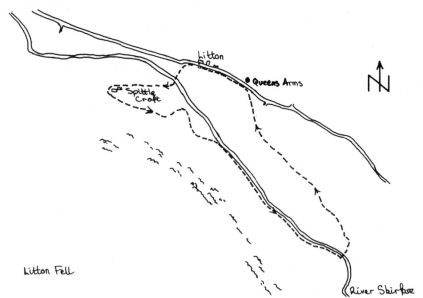

The Queen's Arms in its beautiful setting.

The Walk

Turn right from the inn along the road, passing the post office and Litton Hall. Nearly opposite a telephone box, turn left by a craft shop and cross the dry-bed of the Skirfare on a footbridge.

Bear right across two fields to the back of Spittle Croft. Turn left on a descending path to the river bed and continue along the footpath signposted to 'Arncliffe' for ¾ mile to a point where a loop in the river bed ends. Cross here (in exceptionally wet weather you may need a canoe) and turn left, following the well marked footpath back to Litton and the Queen's Arms.

Other local attractions: Kilnsey Crag and Trout Farm (fishing).

Bolton Percy
The Crown

At the Crown, in the soporific hamlet of Bolton Percy, the term 'a relaxing drink' takes on a new meaning. This establishment, blessed by geography with a glorious isolation, provides excellent Samuel Smith bitter, 10oz sirloin steaks and luscious kebabs for DIY grilling on Saturday barbecue nights. There is a full range of lunchtime and evening bar meals, and for special occasions, a hedonistic gourmet menu which boasts scampi royale, fillet of beef chasseur, roast duckling and pheasant and raspberry pavlova.

A rosy-bricked building, in the shadow of a medieval gatehouse and the historic church of All Saints, the Crown sparkles with brasses and winter fireglow, but is almost deserted on summer afternoons. Spilling down to a stream patrolled by ducks and dragonflies, the blossom-shaded patio is the most palatable cure for indigestion in Yorkshire. Even inclement weather fails to dampen the appetite. On wet nights, diners may retire to the old barn, which is also available for party bookings.

The landlord, with his wife, dispenses addictive prescriptions for the city blues from Monday to Friday 10.30 am to 3 pm and 6.30 pm to 11 pm, Saturday all day, and Sunday 12 noon to 3 pm and 7 pm to 10.30 pm.

Telephone: 0904 84255.

How to get there: The inn is in the village of Bolton Percy, on a minor road 3 miles south-east of Tadcaster.

Parking: Park in the inn car park.

Length of the walk: 2¼ miles. OS Map Landranger series No. 105 (inn GR 532413).

The ideal antidote for over-indulgence at the Crown, this is a pleasant amble over fields to the tidal river Wharfe. But beware the sleep-inducing lap and gurgle of the water!

The Walk

Leaving the car park, turn right along a metalled road to a junction. Turn right again to a sign marked 'Private Road – Bolton Lodge' and fork left along a track. Mounting a stile on the right, bear diagonally left across a field to a second stile and walk field-side to a point

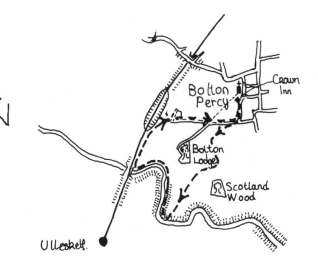

equidistant between two woods. Turn right across a field to the apex of a hedge and follow the hedge line right to a third stile and turn left. Cross a fourth stile to the ings meadow and the banks of the Wharfe. Across the meadow, near the prominent snow-white Ship Inn, is the workshop of Wharfedale's last surviving basket maker.

Continue upstream to the railway bridge (a hoard of Anglo-Saxon coins was found near here in 1967) and turn right along the trackside, bearing right away from a cutting along a hedge path to the side of a wood. Proceed along a farm track to rejoin the Bolton Lodge access road and turn left and left again to the inn.

Other local attractions: All Saints church (consecrated in 1424) – see the Jacobean box pews, and in the west end of the chancel, oak stalls with mutilation said to have been caused by Roundhead soldiers when sharpening their swords; Elizabethan sundial in the churchyard. Also a 15th century timber framed gatehouse.

Sheriff Hutton
The Highwayman

Dwarfed by the skeletal remains of Sheriff Hutton Castle, the Highwayman recalls, in its sign and bar-side flintlocks, the more colourful days of travel. With a games room, three separate bar areas and a dining room, all decorated and furnished in a variety of styles, the inn has wide appeal.

Casual diners can select from a standard three course mid-week menu which includes home-made soup, goujons of tuna, chicken kiev, mushroom and nut fettucini and lemon sponge and custard. A daily special alternative features such dishes as beef-in-ale pie, chicken parcels, liver and onions and lasagne. Under the military eyes of regimental ceiling bosses and muralled hussars, a more comprehensive menu is available in the dining area, where crab and vegetable parcels, hot seafood pancake or one of seven other starters can be followed by a volley of steak dishes, duckling with brandy and orange sauce, baked mussels or a chestnut stuffed pine-nut kernel loaf. Sweets are of all calibres, ranging from lemon sorbet to treacle roly-poly with custard. Two hand-pulled bitter beers from Tetley and Younger (No. 3) are offered, together with Tetley Falstaff, Skol, Castlemaine,

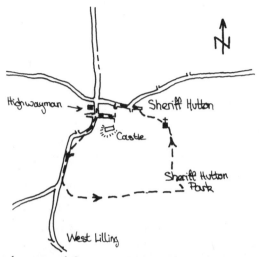

and Lowenbrau lagers and Gaymers Olde English cider. The inn caters for children, providing both adapted meals and a large, safe playing area to the rear.

Opening hours are from Monday (closed Monday lunchtime) to Saturday 11.30 am to 3 pm and 6.30 pm to 11 pm and Sunday 12 noon to 3 pm and 7 pm to 10.30 pm. Formal meals are available from Monday to Saturday (Tuesday to Saturday in winter).

Telephone: 0347 878328.

How to get there: The inn is in the village of Sheriff Hutton north of York.

Parking: Park in the inn car park or in the adjoining lane.

Length of the walk: 2 miles. OS Map Landranger series No. 100 (inn GR 651665).

This is a gentle amble, circuiting the magnificent ruin of Sheriff Hutton castle. There may be opportunities en route for watching a spot of cricket or for falling asleep in the churchyard.

The Walk

Turn right from the inn and walk on a roadside footpath in the direction of West Lilling. Turn left at the road fork along the Sheriff Hutton Park grounds access marked 'Hotel 1 mile'. Continue to the boundary of Sheriff Hutton Hall and turn left by a small lake, continuing through open fields to St. Helen and the Holy Cross churchyard.

Proceed past the church via East End, The Green and the Castle Inn, and turn left to Castle Farm. After 20 yards turn right over a stile into the castle precincts. Cross a second stile to return to your starting point.

Other local attractions: Sheriff Hutton Park (open Monday to Friday only).

Middleham
The Black Swan

This grade II listed 17th century inn stands in a rakish market square on a hillside topped by the ramparts of Richard III's Middleham Castle. At a busy junction of dales roads, Middleham is an ideal base for touring the national park. The town is also noted for its bloodstock and guests at the seven bedroomed Black Swan enjoy a clip-clop reveille.

Served in split-level oak-beamed bars, appropriately hung with horse-racing prints, or in twin dining rooms, meals are both original and freshly made. Alongside popular pies and grills, a number of specialities are offered. These include Wensleydale cheese soup, deep fried camembert and brie wedges, smoked fish platter (consisting of halibut, salmon, mackerel and trout), beef in Old Peculier, pork in Blackthorn cider and highly complimented griddled steaks. Weather permitting, meals can be enjoyed 'al fresco' in the floodlit beer garden to the rear. Children are catered for and dogs are welcome. A Theakston trio – Bitter, XB and Old Peculier – satisfy most thirsts, but John Smith's Keg, Carlsberg lager and Blackthorn Dry and Taunton Sweet ciders are also available.

The inn is open from Monday to Saturday between 11 am and 3 pm and 6 pm and 11 pm. and Sunday from 12 noon to 3 pm and 7 pm to 10.30 pm.
Telephone 0969 22221.

How to get there: The Black Swan is in the market town of Middleham on the A6108.

Parking: Park in the market square.

Length of the walk: 2½ miles. OS Map Outdoor Leisure series No. 30 (inn GR 128878).

A short and easy ramble past the castle to the banks of the river Cover.

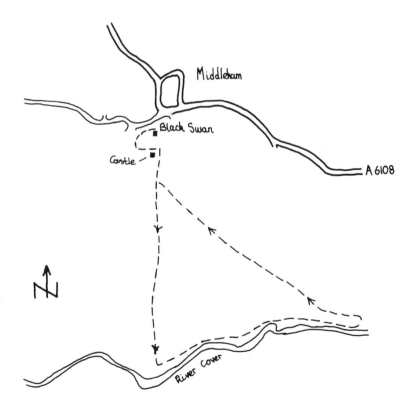

The Walk

Turn left from the inn along the main road and turn left again, passing the entrance to the castle. Turn right along a marked footpath through a gate, continuing wallside to a copse and the river Cover. This was the childhood haunt of the boy destined to become King Richard III.

Turn left along the bank and enter a wood. Continue, emerging from the wood at a deep bend in the river. Bear left across a meadow, heading for an uphill track between flanking belts of trees. Turn sharp left at the top of the track and veer left across a meadow to a gap in a stone wall by a large ash tree. Bear right diagonally to the corner of the next field and march on to the rallying flag-pole of the castle.

Other local attractions: Middleham Castle (English Heritage – admission fee), free show of thoroughbreds exercising on Middleham Moors, and fishing in the Ure and Cover.

Robin Hood's Bay
The Bay

Built on an old staithe, the Bay is licked by the sea with every tide. On the upper decks, the inn has three letting bedrooms and two sea-view bars, one fitted with imaginatively adapted barrels and hung with prints. Below is the flagged and lanterned Stable Bar.

The goal of coast to coast walkers, the Bay provides a wide selection of bar meals, changed daily. The blackboard menu typically lists locally caught mackerel, ling and cod, home-made cottage pie, beef goulash and gammon. Apple and blackcurrant pancake is one of the more popular sweets. Children are welcome. John Smith's hand-pulled bitter and Ruddles County and Courage Directors bitter are available together with Beamish Stout, Foster's and Kronenbourg lagers and Strongbow cider. On special Indian nights during the winter months you may snuggle up to the fire with your vindaloo and eye the waves – very atmospheric!

The inn is open from 11 am to 11 pm Monday to Saturday. Sunday hours are from 12 noon to 3 pm and 7.30 pm to 10.30 pm.

Telephone 0947 880278.

How to get there: The inn is at the bottom of an incredibly steep hill in Robin Hood's Bay.

Parking: There is definitely no parking near the inn but 'pay and display' facilities are available at the top of the hill and in the old station yard.

Length of the walk: 2½ miles. OS Map Outdoor Leisure series No. 27 (inn GR 953048).

A cliff top ramble affording views of a town whose haphazard development and red-roofed jumble is the most compelling argument yet against the need for planning permission.

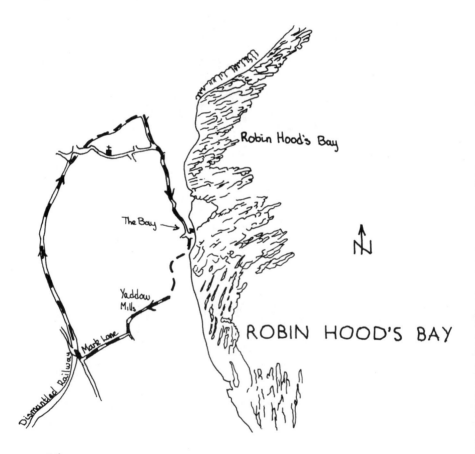

Dramatic Robin Hood's Bay.

The Walk

Take the steps opposite the inn (Covet Hill) and follow the cliff top path towards distant Ravenscar for ½ mile. Turn right away from the sea, crossing a stile, and walk towards Yaddow Mills. Mount a second stile, cross a hardstanding to a third stile and turn left following the 'concessionary path' sign to Mark Lane. Turn right and right again and opposite the private road access to Low Farm take the footpath on your right along the old railway track. (The closure of this line was a short-sighted blunder. Imagine the immense popularity of a modern day haul by The Flying Scotsman between Scarborough and Whitby.) Chug along to the diversion sign and leave the track.

Crossing the road and bearing left, follow the village hall sign through the car park to Mount Pleasant Road. Turn right into Robin Hood's Bay. Do not miss the opportunity of exploring the maze of ginnels and alleyways – look out for Jim Bell's Stile, The Dock and Flagstaff Steps, before returning to the inn.

Other local attractions: A privately run museum of local life, and fossil hunting on the cliffs.

⑪ Filey
The Star

Distinguished by its elegant exterior and romantic sign, The Star caters for visitors to what is Yorkshire's premier family resort. With two attractive bars and its own children's room, the inn offers a menu based on tried and tested Yorkshire recipes. Unsophisticated but hearty and moderately priced, three course bar meals typically begin with home-made soup followed by hot beef sandwiches, steak pie, and chicken and ham pie. Grandmother's well-thumbed notebook similarly inspires the bread and butter pudding, treacle sponge and generous apple pie. Children's portions are available. The Star stocks a wide selection of beers, lagers and stouts – hand-pulled Tetley, Camerons and Whitbread bitters and Russells mild, Skol, Castlemaine and Labatts lagers and draught Guiness. The Star has pleasant outside seating areas to both the front and the rear.

Opening times are from Monday to Saturday 11 am to 11 pm (subject to change in winter). Sunday hours are from 12 noonto 3 pm to 3 pm and 7 pm to 10.30 pm.

Telephone: 0723 512437.

How to get there: The inn is located on Mitford Street near Filey centre.

Parking: Park in the inn car park.

Length of the walk: 2½ miles. OS Map Landranger series No. 101 (inn GR 118808).

Appetite jaded? Need a tonic? Well this is the hike for you, easy but exhilarating. Relish the march to the famous Filey Brigg, a 'Guns of Navarone' type assault on the cliffs and a pilgrimage to the shrine of a fellow pedestrian whose odysseys put our own excursions in the shade. Check the tides before you set off, for the beach at the start of the walk can only be crossed at low water.

The Walk

Turn left from the inn and bear right passing over a pedestrianised seating area to a flight of steps. Descend and bear left on a footpath to the Coble Landing, striding out across the beach (at low tide!) to the jutting reef of Filey Brigg. Bear right along the causeway under the cliffs and begin your climb where the cliffs end (the fixed ropes are all ready for you). At the summit bear left along the cliff edge heading for the distant church tower.

Descend a ravine (the access road to the Filey Yacht Club) and turn right uphill, turning left by the Country Park Stores to the Filey Brigg

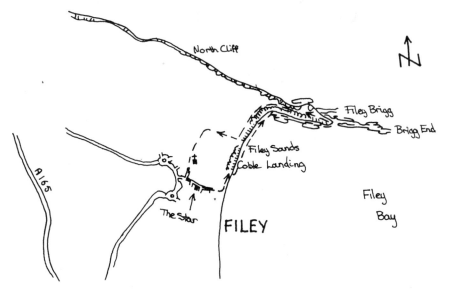

caravan park exit. Follow the road to the right, turn left and go left again to the back of St. Oswald's church. The celebrated 'Walking Parson', Arthur Neville Cooper, was canon at Filey until his death in 1880. You can see his memorial stone in the chancel, 'They that wait upon the Lord shall renew their strength, they shall walk and not faint', and you might want to read the parson's books 'Quaint Talks About Long Walks' and 'With Knapsack and Notebook'.

Leave the church by the front porch and bear left over a footbridge. Bear right by the Station inn and Christmas Cottage and turn left on Mitford Street back to The Star.

Other local attractions: Filey Museum.

Aldborough
The Ship

Centred around a village green with its stocks and maypole, the pretty village of Aldborough has dozed since the Roman legions left. Once the site of the Roman town of Isurium Brigantum, Aldborough has many ancient attractions, not least the inviting Ship Inn whose proximity to a strategic crossing of the Ure explains the jaunty name. The connection with ships extends well beyond the threshold into an inglenooked bar, beamed with man-of-war timbers, the below decks atmosphere heightened by a flotsam collection of odd chairs. Together with a ship's wheel and sea prints in the adjoining dining area, the inn has everything but the spray.

Bar meals and more substantial three course repasts are available daily, the standard menu being supplemented by a daily special. Lamb cutlets, chicken Kiev, giant Yorkshire puddings and open-top sandwiches account for a busy lunchtime trade. More leisured diners can choose from grilled sardines with lemon, smoked salmon rolls stuffed with prawns, melon balls with fresh ginger, an exotically presented range of fish dishes which includes fillet of plaice in a banana, cashew nut and cream sauce, and specialities such as fillet of

41

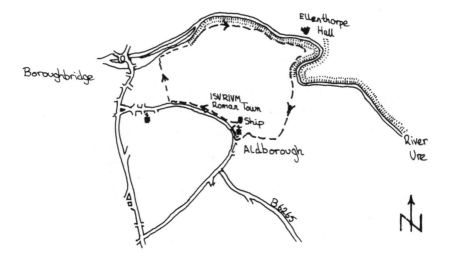

veal, rack of lamb, roast duck and supreme of chicken flambé with whiskey in an almond and cream sauce. The inn has a good selection of hand-pulled ales – John Smith, Worthingtons, Tetley and Theakston bitters, Tetley Mild, together with Foster's, Coors and Carlsberg lagers and Murphy's and Gillespie stouts. Accommodation is provided in five letting rooms.

Opening times are from Monday to Friday 12 noon to 2.30 pm and 5.45 pm to 11 pm; Saturday 12 noon to 3 pm and 5.45 pm to 11 pm and Sunday from 12 noon to 3 pm and 7 pm to 10.30 pm.

Telephone: 0423 322749.

How to get there: The inn is opposite St. Andrew's church in the village of Aldborough near Boroughbridge.

Parking: Park in the inn car park.

Length of the walk: 2½ miles. OS Map Landranger series No. 99 (inn GR 405664).

A gentle stroll along the banks of the Ure with opportunities on summer Sundays to witness the rituals of match fishing.

42

The Walk

Turn right from the inn along the road (the 'via principalis' or central axis of the Roman town) in the direction of Boroughbridge, passing the village cross on your left. Leave the village and, opposite the school playing fields on a bend, turn right along a footpath to the river.

Turn right, following the river bank to a stile and a sign marked 'Match Limit'. Continue, passing Ellenthorpe Hall on the far bank. The triffids have nothing on the unmistakable weeds sprouting here. Once grown for its decorative qualities, the giant hogweed has since colonised this area, and you should be warned that contact with the plant can cause serious skin problems.

Follow the reversed 'S' river bend round to a sign marked 'Leeds Amalgamation'. Turn right along a track into Aldborough. Turn right again and go first left to the village green, walking around the back of the church to the inn.

Other local attractions: Alborough Roman Town (fine mosaics and artefacts – admission fee, closed on Mondays October to March), St. Andrew's church, and an incredible pie-shop in Boroughbridge.

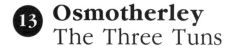

Osmotherley
The Three Tuns

In a village made famous by the gruelling 42 mile Lyke Wake Walk, the Three Tuns dispenses the choicest last rites. Known locally as the 'Mousehole', the inn has a cosy low beamed interior.

Changed daily, the menu, based on fresh local produce, is adventurous even by restaurant standards. Meals typically begin with California pepperpot, lettuce or Stilton and onion soup, followed in season by main courses such as venison, lobster, lemon sole, pheasant and grouse. Beef en croute, roast breast of Barbary duck with blackcurrant and port sauce, salmon and plaice parcels with crab sauce, rack of lamb and summer chicken (stuffed with cheese, pine nuts and an asparagus sauce) are generally available throughout the year. Sweets range from rhubarb and orange crumble and bread and butter pudding to strawberry and whisky trifle and American lemon gateau. Children are welcome. There is a choice of hand-pulled ales – Younger No. 3, Theakston Bitter, XB and Old Peculier and McEwan 80/-. Carlsberg and Becks lagers and Autum Gold cider are also on tap.

The inn has a relaxing floral beer garden at the rear and is open from Monday to Saturday 12 noon to 3.30 pm and 7 pm to 11 pm. Sunday hours are from 12 noon to 3 pm and 7 pm to 10.30 pm.

Telephone: 0609 883301.

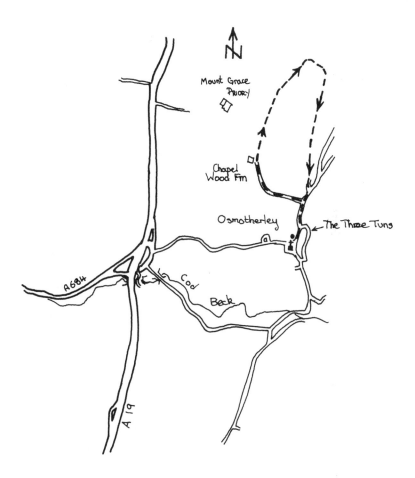

How to get there: The inn is in the village of Osmotherley near Northallerton.

Parking: Park in front of the inn or on the street.

Length of the walk: 2½ miles. OS Map Landranger series No. 99 (inn GR 457973).

Save the Lyke Wake Walk for another day (it runs between Osmotherley and Ravenscar on the coast) and take this relaxing amble, discovering a shrine that has attracted pilgrims for centuries, and the ingredients for a bilberry pie.

The Walk

Turn right from the inn, passing the village green on the road to Swainby. Turn left along Ruebury Lane on a footpath signposted 'Cleveland Way'. Climb the hill and look out for a fork on your right, turning right along the access track to a chapel – the Shrine of Our Lady of Mount Grace, 16th century place of pilgrimage after the Reformation. The view from the site is superb.

Go back to the fork (notice the toposcope?) and turn right, passing Chapel Wood Farm. Continue on to Arncliffe Wood and take the right-hand fork uphill. Bilberries! The bushes were dripping with them when I came this way. They make the most scrumptious pies in the world, and if you come in August you may pick away at your leisure and still have time for the pub.

Proceed to a 'moonbase' sprouting aerial dishes and antennae – a microwave radio station. Turn right, away from the station on the access track. To the left you will see the pappy eminence of Roseberry Topping: to the right is the mass of Black Hambledon. Swing right and continue downhill to the road. Turn right into Osmotherley.

Other local attractions: Osmotherley's public conveniences (voted the 'Top Loo in Britain') and Mount Grace Priory.

Whitby
The Duke of York

Commanding panoramic views of Whitby harbour, the Duke of York allows you to quaff and watch your lunch sail by. This ancient haunt of smugglers specialises in fresh crab salads served from a refrigerated display in the bar. Scampi, haddock, mackerel, prawns and squid rings are also available alongside an international selection of dishes which includes steak and kidney pie, roast ham, quiche, chicken tikka, chilli con carne and vegetable stroganoff accompanied by naan bread and tortilla chips. Children are catered for. The grog shop offers hand-pulled John Smith Bitter, Magnet, and Courage Directors (together with a cosmopolitan tally of bottled beers), Guiness, Carlsberg and Kronenbourg lagers and Red Rock, Scrumpy Jack and Strongbow ciders.

The inn has three letting bedrooms (accommodation only) and is open during the summer months from Monday to Friday 11 am to 11 pm (generally 12 noon to 3 pm and 6 pm to 11 pm in winter). Sunday hours are from 12 noon to 3 pm and 7 pm to 10.30 pm.

Telephone 0947 600324.

WHITBY

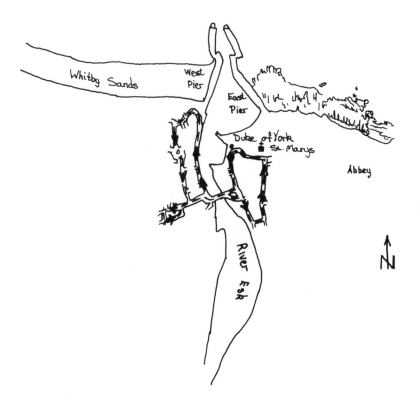

How to get there: The harbourside inn is on Church Street in Whitby.

Parking: Park in the extensive 'pay and display' car park at the back of the railway station.

Length of the walk: 1½ miles. OS Map Outdoor Leisure series No. 27 (inn GR 900114).

Proper exploration is the preserve of the boot, a fact atmospherically demonstrated in this short, footloose tour of old Whitby. Captain Cook, Saint Hilda, Count Dracula and a myriad other sea-soused souls haunt this place.

The Walk

Start at the bottom of the famous 199 steps on Church Street. (You are at the spot where Count Dracula, newly arrived by sea from Transylvania, changed himself into a dog and evaded capture.) Turn right along the cobbled Henrietta Street (inspecting the old yards) and turn right again at Bridge Street, crossing the Esk. Turn right along St. Anns Staith, and continue via Marine Parade, with its fish quay, and Pier Road to the lifeboat station. Turn left up the oddly named Kyber Pass and, crossing the road, climb the bank on a footpath leading to East Terrace. Captain Cook's statue and a monumental testimony to Whitby's whaling industry are sited here.

Turn left and bear left across East Crescent to Cliff Street. Turn right to Flowergate. Turn right to Brunswick Street and turn left to Brunswick churchyard, cutting through the grounds to Baxtergate (more old yards). Turn left and re-cross the Esk on Bridge Street. Turn right along Grape Lane (Cook was billeted here as a lad) and turn right for 150 yards along Church Street. Opposite a car park, cross the road and take a stepped footpath via flats to the back of Elbow Terrace. Turn left to St. Mary's church. Descend via the 199 steps (bridegrooms have been known to wilt after tackling this lot) to the inn.

Other local attractions: Whitby Abbey, The Dracula Experience, deep sea fishing, and Whitby jet.

15 Snape
The Castle Arms

Classically English, its castle and rose-clad cottages embowering an extensive village green, Snape has all the ingredients for a lazy afternoon. Challenging its namesake for antiquity, the Castle Arms is a homely inn, providing accommodation (two bedrooms), real ale and good food, served either in the open-fired bar or the dining room.

Revealing the cosmopolitan bent of the cook, international spice enlivens the goulash soup, crispy coated camembert and vegetable samosa starters. Main courses also break ethnic ground, offering Cumberland sausage, Raj vegetable curry, moussaka, rabbit chasseur, cottage pie, country lentil crumble, pheasant chasseur, and, the speciality of the house, castle pie, a combination of steak, red and green peppers and onions. Reminiscent of an Austrian hunting lodge, the stone-flagged dining room visibly complements the menu with a rare assembly of old frying pans, thimbles and chamois antlers. Children are welcome. Three real, hand-pulled ales – Hambleton, Tetley and John Smith – are served alongside Carlsberg lager, Beamish Stout and Dry Blackthorn cider. To the rear the inn has facilities for camping and caravanning (registered site).

Opening hours are from Monday (but closed Monday lunchtime) to Saturday 12 noon to 3 pm and 6 pm to 11 pm. Sunday hours are from 12 noon to 3 pm and 7 pm to 10.30 pm.

Telephone 0677 70270.

How to get there: The inn is in the village of Snape, south of Bedale.

Parking: Park outside the inn, or on the street.

Length of the walk: 4½ miles. OS Map Landranger series No. 99 (inn GR 267843).

A pleasant and untaxing walk (without a contour) over meadows and woodland tracks. The route can be boggy in places.

The Walk

Immediately to the right of the inn, take a track, walking north alongside woodland. Bear right (Thorp Perrow house is viewed to the left) and turn left, on a footpath skirting the edge of a field used for

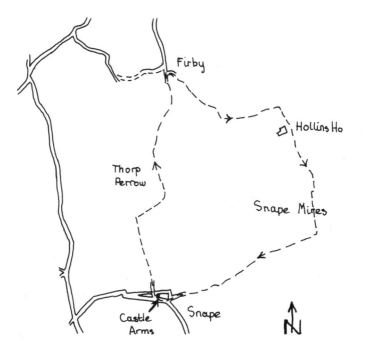

turf culture. Continue (do not deviate to the right) and go through two waymarked gates to enter pastureland containing specimen oaks. Go forward, bearing left by the bungalow to an access road. Turn right, go through white gates and continue over two bridges. Pass Firby Lodge to Firby.

Turn right at Firby House, through a farmyard and follow the snaking road to Hollins House. Continue straight on to a gate, whose top bar is painted white. Adjacent to this you will see a hurdle – or could it be described as a stile? (The OS Map shows public rights of way hereabouts. Ignore them. The farmer has devised an interesting hide-and-seek detour.) Turn right into the field, walking behind a conifer hedge and go straight forward to the edge of a copse. Continue along the copse side and cross a ditch via a bridge between double gates. Veer right to the edge of woodland in Snape Mires and continue over boggy ground to join Mires Farm access track. Turn right along the track to return to Snape.

Other local attractions: Thorp Perrow arboretum (best seen in spring and autumn).

Cloughton
16
The Blacksmith's Arms

This inviting roadside inn is tradition itself, offering low beams, a wealth of scuttles, brasses and copper kettles and an inglenook which is perfect for toasting chilblains. Best seen to advantage in winter, two plush bars serve home-cooked meals both lunchtime and evening.

Grilled steaks, hot sirloin sandwiches, fresh plaice and haddock and smoked salmon sandwiches are very popular, or you could opt for meat and potato pies, beef curries and Yorkshire puddings with onion gravy. There is a separate menu for children and a formal restaurant serving speciality soups, crunchy waldorf salad, chicken stilton, duckling, escalope of veal, and fillet steak with prawns, pan-fried in butter and flambéd in brandy and cream. Worthing Bitter, Bass Light and Bass Mild, Stones Bitter, Tennent and Carling Black Label lager and Guinness are available on draught.

The inn has six letting bedrooms and is open from Monday to Saturday 11 am to 3 pm and 6.30 pm to 11 pm. Sunday hours are from 12 noon to 3 pm and 7 pm to 10.30 pm.

Telephone 0723 870244.

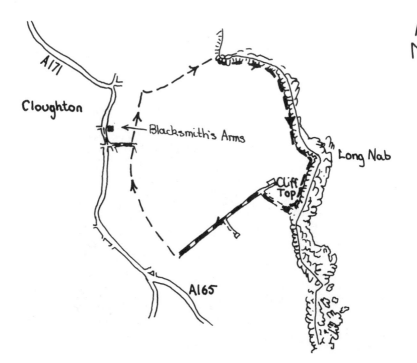

How to get there: The inn is in the village of Cloughton, fronting the main A171 Scarborough to Whitby road.

Parking: Park in the inn car park. A word of warning: heed the sign and do not leave the car park by the left hand exit. The lack of visibility makes the manoeuvre dangerous.

Length of the walk: 5½ miles. OS Map Landranger series No. 101 (inn GR 009943).

An invigorating cliff top ramble (the ravines entail some heavy breathing). Terrific for a winter's day.

The Walk

Turn left from the inn along the A171 and pass the church. Turn left along the residential Station Lane and, opposite the old railway station and yard, turn left along the redundant railway track. Continue to an overbridge, turn left up the embankment and turn left again onto the bridge, walking on towards the sea. Scarborough Castle comes into view on your right; Hayburn Wyke Woods to your left.

Turn right on a see-saw path for 1 mile. See if you can spot the clifftop stakes of old 'climmers' along the way. The business of collecting birds eggs for food and patent leather processing only became illegal in 1954. Walk on from the Long Nab Coastguard Station to Crook Ness and, ignoring the path to the left, turn right on a road in the direction of Cliff Top House. Turn left along the farm access road to a railway bridge and turn left up the embankment and left again along the old track to the former railway station. Turn left to the A171 and the inn.

Other local attractions: National Trust woodland and waterfall at Hayburn Wyke.

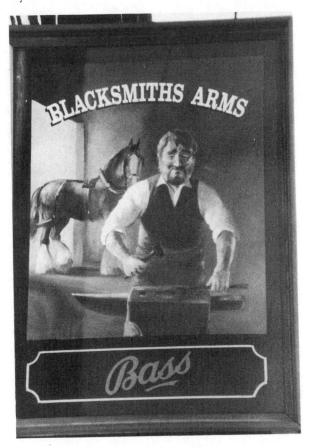

17 Carlton Husthwaite
The Carlton

In an area famous for bloodstock, the Carlton is one of the most welcoming of inns. Candles flicker both lunchtime and evening in a plush bar, unusually decorated with racecourse ring badges, inviting customers to sample a wide range of bar and dining room meals.

Changed daily, the freshly made and generously portioned fare features ham cornet, salmon in parsley sauce, grilled Yorkshire gammon, ragout of lamb, chicken Hawaii (sauced in an orange, peach, pineapple, herb, onion and sherry mixture), creamed halibut, and hot-pot with ale, topped with saute potatoes. The range of ten vegetarian dishes boasts bubble and squeak medallions. The line-up of sweets includes toffee-coffee pie, ginger sponge, Malibu and coconut slice and banoffi tart. Children are welcome. Hand-pulled Tetley and William Younger Bitter are available together with Lowenbrau and Castlemaine lagers and draught Guinness. There is an adjoining games room and an adjacent beer garden/children's play area.

The inn has a registered caravan site to the rear, and is open from Wednesday to Saturday 11 am to 3 pm and 7 pm to 11 pm (open evenings only on Monday and Tuesday). Sunday hours are from 12 noon to 3 pm and 7 pm to 10.30 pm.

Telephone: 0845 401265.

How to get there: The inn is in the village of Carlton Husthwaite off the A19 between Easingwold and Thirsk.

Parking: Park in the inn car park.

Length of the walk: 4½ miles. OS Map Landranger series No. 100 (inn GR 497767).

A gentle circuit over tracks and fields between the two Husthwaites, stalking the famous White Horse of Kilburn.

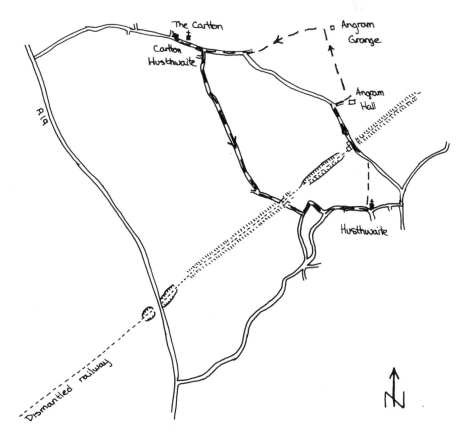

The Walk

Turn left from the inn through Carlton Husthwaite, noticing the thatched timber framed house opposite the hall. At the end of the village, beyond the house called The End, turn right on a track leading to a microlight aircraft hangar and landing strip. Continue under a railway bridge and cross Elphin Beck. Bear left and then right into Husthwaite.

Turn right along the main street past the Blacksmith's Arms to St. Nicholas' Norman church. If you would care to enter, here's a puzzle for you. Find a squint. It has something to do with the eyes.

Take the footpath at the side of the church, follow it as it zig-zags round the back of a garage, cross a paddock to a stile and continue downhill along a field side. The White Horse of Kilburn dominates the horizon. Turn left at the road, recross the Elphin Beck and turn right on the access to Angram Hall. Go left through the farmyard and continue straight on through red tubular gates. Veering left across a field, cross a ditch on sleepers to a second gate. Proceed uphill steering left of Angram Grange to the top of the field. Turn left along the hedge line passing through two gates to a path between hedgerows. Walk on to the road and turn right to the village and back to the inn.

Other local attractions: Malcolm Pipes, a specialist in English oak furniture (workshops and showroom in the village).

18 Oldstead
The Black Swan

The Black Swan is tranquillity unfurled. Spacious and airy, the inn has an elevated restaurant and a lower part-flagged bar, handsomely fitted with oak from the celebrated 'Mouseman' Thompson workshops close by.

Large bow windows embracing open fields make for relaxed eating. Home-made soup with a hunk of cheese heralds a substantial bar menu, which lists hot French bread with home-cooked ham in cider, 'surf and turf' (scampi and fillet steak), lasagne, moussaka, game pie and 'grunt and flutter' (wild boar and pheasant) and a range of vegetarian and vegan dishes including chilli chickpea crumble. Restaurant diners may choose from seafood bouche, tarragon chicken, pork in apricot brandy, sirloin and fillet steak, beef wellington and tagliatelle carbonara. Children are welcome. Hand-pulled Theakston, John Smith and Tetley bitters, Beamish Stout, Foster's and Carlsberg lagers and Woodpecker cider compete alongside an extensive wine list. The inn has six letting bedrooms and a shady front terrace.

Opening times are from Monday to Saturday 12 noon to 2.30 pm

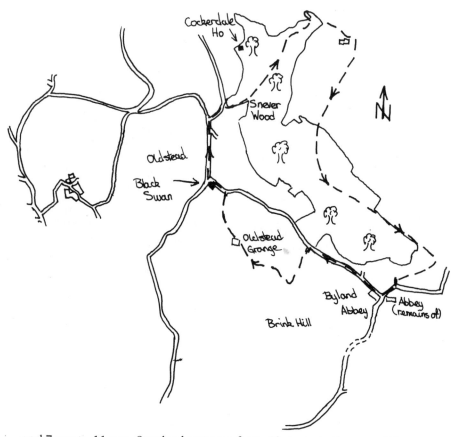

and 7 pm to 11 pm. Sunday hours are from 12 noon to 3 pm and 7 pm to 10.30 pm.

Telephone: 0347 868387.

How to get there: The inn is on the edge of the sleepy village of Oldstead, south of the A170 and Sutton Bank.

Parking: Park in the inn car park.

Length of the walk: 5 miles. OS Map Landranger series No. 100 (inn GR 531799).

A refreshing ramble, visiting pine woods, meadows and a slumbering abbey.

60

The Walk

From the inn walk northward through the village on the road to Kilburn. Leaving the village at the start of the bend in the road, take the track on your right (signposted as a dead end) and walk to a fork. Take the right-hand track signposted to Cockerdale House and proceed uphill. This is quite a steep climb. Bear right into Snever Wood. After two descents (and rises!) swing right to leave the wood. Continue through two gates to Cam Farm. Turn right by the farmhouse boundary wall (no sign) and continue over the meadow to a gate. Here you will find an old overgrown wall. Follow it down and re-enter Snever Wood.

Go straight on bearing left downhill. Fork left uphill by a pheasantry, and turn right, leaving the wood and following a footpath sign. Steer right across the field, dropping down to the edge of the wood towards a kissing gate. Continue on a track for 200 yards and turn right along a footpath signposted to the 12th century Byland Abbey (in the care of English Heritage – admission fee).

Turn right along the road and turn right again by the Abbey Inn in the direction of Oldstead. Continue under the remains of the old gatehouse along the quiet road for ½ mile to a track on the left. Turn left heading towards Brink Hill. Where the track bends keep straight on for 20 yards and turn right along the footpath signposted to Oldstead Grange. Proceed through the farmyard (you'll get a fleeting glimpse of the White Horse of Kilburn at this point) to rejoin the road. Turn left back to the inn.

Other local attractions: The White Horse of Kilburn and the Kilburn workshops and showrooms of 'Mouseman' Thompson.

19 Ravensworth
The Bay Horse

Encircling a Wembley of turf, the village of Ravensworth has a ruined castle, a ring of stone cottages and yawning skies. The 18th century Bay Horse stands by the roadside, a bluff stone building offering two small bars and a dining room. Hung with evocative photographs, alongside a collection of brasses, tankards, beer-mats and old clogs, the inn serves standard lunchtime and evening fare together with daily specials. Starters feature garlic mushrooms with hot toast, Yorkshire puddings and corn-on-the-cob. The main course menu lists gourmet scampi, pork chop, home-made steak and kidney pie, Barnsley chop, T-bone steak and roast duckling. Blackboard specials, which vary according to the season, include such dishes as poussin with mangetout peas and steak and ale pie. Children are welcome. Tetley, McEwans 80/-, Hambleton and Theakston hand-pulled ales are available alongside 'guest' beers and Carlsberg and Lowenbrau lagers. Liqueur coffees are a speciality of the house.

Opening times are from Monday to Saturday 11 am to 3 pm and 7 pm to 11 pm. Sunday hours are from 12 noon to 3 pm and 7 pm to 10.30 pm.

Telephone: 0325 718328.

How to get there: The inn is in the village of Ravensworth north of Richmond.

Parking: Park by the village green.

Length of the walk: 4½ miles. OS Map Landranger series No. 92 (inn GR 140082).

This panoramic circuit offers perfect peace, (the MOD ranges are well to the south), and the ruins of an ancient castle.

The Walk
Turn right from the inn on the road to Gayles. Pass the school and where the road bends continue straight on through a blue gate marked 'Larklands' towards semi-derelict farmbuildings on the hill. The public right-of-way is indeterminate at this point. Go left through a gate and ascend to the farmbuildings going right, through the old farmyard to another gate.

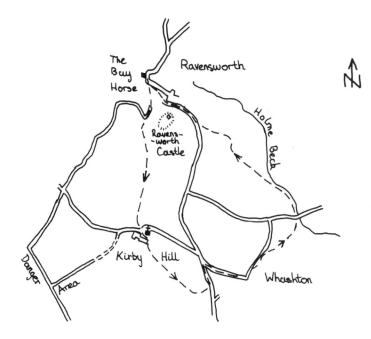

Turn left over the pasture, heading diagonally across to a further gate and go left at the bottom of hummocky ground to yet another gate. Climb Kirby Hill heading between rocky projections to find a crossing in the wall. Cross into a small field and turn right to the Shoulder of Mutton inn. Turn left and left again, passing the church and turning right in the far corner of the square on a track between Rose Cottage and Holm Garth. Keeping in the bottom with a pond to your left, continue on the track to the road, and turn left and right following the signpost to Whashton.

Turn left by the Hack and Spade inn and drop down to a white tubular gate on your right. Go through and veer left in an arc downhill to the Holme Beck and a white gate. Turn left by the bridge for 10 yards only and take the waymarked footpath on your right upstream. Bear left across the fourth field (if it is in crop go round) to a stile over a wall and go left, heading towards the field taper and a stockade. Continue along a track to the road and turn right, passing the ruins of Ravensworth Castle, to the village.

Other local attractions: Richmond.

Glaisdale
The Anglers Rest

A former farm and alehouse in a valley surrounded by ear-popping hills, the Anglers Rest is now a popular country inn. Originally called the 'Three Blast Furnaces' in reference to a local foundry (the landlord objected to receiving mail addressed to 'The Three BFs'), the inn offers comprehensive facilities which include four letting bedrooms and a dining room, a camping ground and 'outward bound' type courses for teenagers. Maps are available on free loan.

Hung with photographs of local scenes, the rustic bar serves a good selection of home-cooked meals – steak and kidney pie cooked in Guinness, roast lamb, beef and pork, chicken tikka, omelettes and a wide range of snacks. Vegetarians can enjoy savoury stuffed pancakes, shepherds spicy lentil pie and veggie hot-pot. The converted cow-byre dining room offers grilled grapefruit glacé, Yorkshire pudding with onion gravy, beef steak kebabs, tournados rossini, grilled prawns in bacon, lobster julien and trout with prawns. Children are welcome. Three hand-pulled real ales – Tetley, Theakston Bitter and Old Peculier – are well presented, alongside draught Guinness and Carlsberg and Labatts lagers.

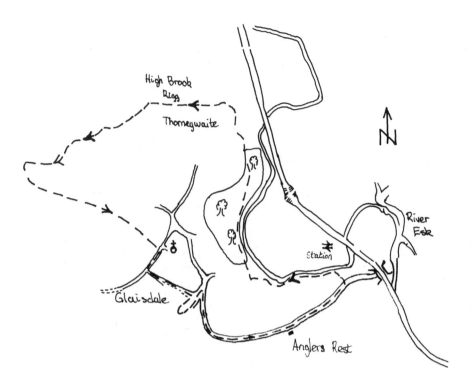

The inn has a rear beer garden and is open from Monday to Saturday 11 am to 2.30 pm and 7 pm to 11 pm. Sunday hours from 12 noon to 3 pm and 7.30 pm to 10.30 pm.
Telephone: 0947 87261.

How to get there: The inn is in the village of Glaisdale in the North York Moors National Park.

Parking: Park in the inn car park.

Length of the walk: 5 miles. OS Map Outdoor Leisure sries No. 27 (inn GR 781053).

A pleasant undulating ramble by the river Esk, through meadows and woods.

The Walk

Turn right from the inn downhill and turn left along the road signposted 'local traffic only'. Cross a bridge and swing left up a steep hill. Near the crest take a footpath on your right into Millers Wood. Follow the Esk upstream, bearing left by a cottage. Continue uphill and leave the wood, swinging left to the lawn of a house named Thorneywaite. Cross the lawn and mount a ladder stile onto a road.

Turn left for 20 yards and turn right on a footpath to the group of buildings at High Brook Rigg. Go straight on, through a gate to your right and turn left immediately following a curving path (first between two fields and then through bracken) to a track. Turn right, passing a line of cottages to the road. Turn left uphill over a bridge and continue to the Glaisdale sign.

Turn right opposite this sign and turn left along the wallside over a series of ladder stiles to a coalyard. Continue to the road and turn right, passing Montheath and Glaisdale Hall. Turn left over a wall and steer left in the second field to a gate in the corner. Turn right and drop down to the road by the church. Turn right on the road by Parliament Cottage access and turn left by the church. Turn right again, dropping downhill to the tennis courts and continue round the bend and onward to the inn.

Other local attractions: Beggars Bridge over the Esk (dated 1619).

Scarborough
The Albion

21

Dominated by a towering castle keep, the Albion is one of Scarborough's less boisterous inns. In a quiet street opposite the church of St. Mary, the inn offers two comfortable bars, the emphasis being on relaxation and entertainment. Tourists can enjoy live music during the summer season and a local folk club and an Irish vocal society meet at the inn throughout the year. The inn has an interesting collection of military headgear.

Cosmopolitan bar meals, which are served both lunchtime and evening, include chilli con carne, beef curry, moussaka, lasagne and home-cooked ham. Fresh locally caught lemon sole is a speciality. Cameron's is the hand-pulled house bitter, complemented by Strongarm, hand-pulled Tetley Bitter, Murphy's Stout, Skol, Castlemaine and Hansa lagers and Autumn Gold cider. Children are only allowed in the games room.

Opening times from Monday to Saturday are from 12 noon to 4 pm (longer if trade is brisk) and 7 pm to 12 midnight. Sunday opening is from 12 noon to 3 pm and 7.30 pm to 10.30 pm.

Telephone: 0723 379068.

How to get there: The inn is on Castle Road within easy reach of Scarborough's North and South Bays.

Parking: During the holiday season parking is a great problem in Scarborough. Park on street or use the 'pay and display' facilities (long stay) on Royal Albert Drive or Marine Drive.

Length of the walk: 4½ miles. OS Map Landranger series No. 101 (inn GR 047892).

This is a wonderfully varied seaside circuit with a great deal of interest along the way, from Ann Bronte's grave to the Sea Life Centre.

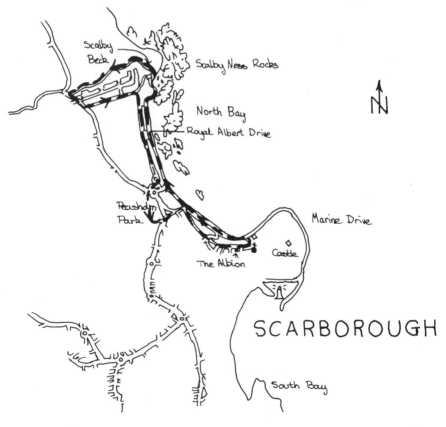

The Walk

Turn left from the inn, passing St. Mary's church (Ann Bronte's grave is here). Turn left by Mulgrave Terrace. The eccentric Castle-By-The-Sea on the right was once owned by the talented artist Atkinson Grimshaw. Turn right, descending long flights of steps to Royal Albert Drive.

Turn left, following the sweep of the bay past the Corner Cafe and on towards distant pyramids at Scalby Mills (the futuristic buildings house Scarborough Sea Life Centre). Passing the Centre, swing left by the footbridge and walk on uphill for 60 yards to the lamp-post numbered 22. Turn right on a footpath uphill and at the crest, bear left to the beck side. The Scalby Beck is a veritable Eden of wild flowers.

Continue upstream to a road bridge and turn left just before the Scarborough sign on a footpath, passing a garage and the Ivanhoe public house. Turn left on Scalby Mills Road. Turn right before the descent, following a footpath signposted 'Peasholm Park and Corner Cafe'.

Turn left on a footbridge crossing the miniature railway. Here you may opt for an alternative mode of travel and take the cable car to Peasholm Park. Alternatively, turn right, passing boating lakes and Peasholm station to the road and the park access. Enter the park and turn left by the lakeside, continuing to the boat hire kiosk. Take the second left and leave the park, turning left on Victoria Road. Cross the junction with Peasholm Road and pass the Alexandra Bowls Centre to the cliff top. Turn right on Queens Parade, and bear left by the Boston Hotel back to the inn.

Other local attractions: After all that exertion I recommend a short cruise. Two well equipped vessels operate from the harbour.

Richmond
The Buck

Dominated by its castle, the market town of Richmond is a popular tourist haunt. Away from the bustle, the Buck can be found on the cobbled and tree-lined Newbiggin, a quiet and attractive inn, advertising its wares to coast to coast walkers.

The Buck serves no bar meals (a fish and chip shop and numerous cafes are close by) but offers a selection of hand-pulled real ales and free entry into a display of 'all our yesterdays' memorabilia (landlords with nervous twitches shouldn't attend auctions) that would put many museums to shame. Every shelf, every ledge, every inch of wall space in the two bars is occupied by tin-plate signs, old radios, typewriters and cameras and a thousand and one other treasures. And the Buck is a must for real brew fans, serving Newcastle Exhibition, Theakston XB and Old Peculier and Younger Scotch bitters, Carlsberg, McEwan and Becks lagers, Guinness and Taunton and Dry Blackthorn ciders. Sip away and see how many trinkets you can recall with your eyes shut. Bed and breakfast is provided for walkers (six rooms), the 'all mod cons' extending to a properly surveyed brass grid point fixed to the bar (it is useful to know when you've had a few that you're exactly 415 ft 7 ½ inches above sea level). Children are welcome and the inn has a relaxing rear beer garden.

RICHMOND

Opening hours are from Monday to Friday 11.30 am to 2.30 pm and 6.30 pm to 11 pm. Saturday hours are from 11.30 am to 11 pm. Sunday opening is from 12 noon to 3 pm and 7 pm to 10.30 pm. Telephone: 0748 822259.

How to get there: The inn is in the market town of Richmond, on Newbiggin near the RC church of St. Joseph.

Parking: Park on Newbiggin or in Market Place.

Length of the walk: 6½ miles. OS Map Landranger series No. 92 (inn GR 168009).

This pleasant walk gives you views of the river Swale from the river bank and from high on Whitecliffe Scar. One steep ascent over scree is involved and boots are advisable.

The Walk

Turn right from the inn along Newbiggin and turn right again down Finkle Street. Emerge into Market Place and cross the square diagonally to the right of the church. Turn right, dropping down Millgate to Castle Walk on your right. Skirt the castle walls and descend to the river.

Cross the bridge and turn right upstream through woodland for 1 mile to a footbridge. Recross the river and bear left by a car park to the road. Turn left, cross to the opposite pavement and 150 yards past the 'Private Woodland' sign take the track on your right to a farmstead. Divert as waymarked, turning right and left into a wood.

Follow the river along a well waymarked path for 1½ miles. Swing right uphill away from the river, pass a derelict barn and go round the front of 'Applegarth' to a gate. Turn right and turn right again over a stile onto a steep road. Past the 'coast to coast' sign, fork left and walk on to find a rough track on your right. Ascend Whitecliffe Scar, taking care over loose scree.

At the summit follow the ridge line through bracken and continue on a well defined path. Pass the monuments at a viewpoint known as Willances Leap. In 1606 Robert Willance was on a hunting trip when his horse accidently leapt over the precipice in thick fog. The horse was killed but its rider survived the 200 ft fall, only suffering a broken leg.

Walk on, eventually veering right towards a farmstead. Turn left through a green gate, continue on to a white gate and follow the signpost marking the coast to coast walk, on a road into Richmond. Turn right down Cravengate and turn left to Newbiggin and the inn.

Other local attractions: Richmond Castle and the Green Howards Museum.

Farndale
The Feversham Arms

23

As remote, but as welcoming a hostelry as can be found in the whole of Yorkshire, the Feversham Arms will be well known to daffodil devotees who flock to Farndale in early spring.

Essentially a farmhouse kitchen with pumps, the bar of the Feversham serves hand-pulled Tetley Bitter, Castlemaine lager and Gaymers Olde English cider, together with a range of fresh and generous bar meals. Pork chops, topside of beef sandwiches, home-made steak and kidney pie, bacon chops, local chicken and a lunch to satisfy a team of ploughmen are all popular, and children's portions are available. In contrast to the flagstoned, black-leaded ruggedness of the bar, an adjacent dining room has been created from what was once a slaughterhouse. In perfect peace, here you can enjoy home-made soup, hot prawns in cheese sauce, fillet of halibut, pork fillet en croute (a speciality), sole veronique, Mexican chicken (with white wine, cream, onions, peppers, mushrooms, chilli, tomatoes and black olives) and fillet steak.

The inn has two letting bedrooms and a small beer garden and is open from Monday to Saturday from 11 am to 3 pm and 6 pm to 11 pm, and Sunday from 12 noon to 3 pm and 7 pm to 10.30 pm.

Telephone: 0751 33206.

The Feversham Arms.

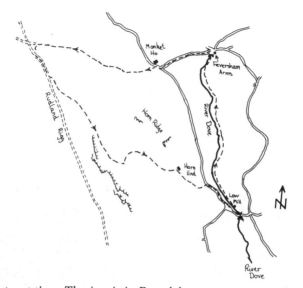

How to get there: The inn is in Farndale, more a geographical area than a settlement in the conventional sense. It lies in the valley of the Dove, 10 miles north of the A170 and Kirkbymoorside.

Parking: Park in the car park to the rear of the inn.

Length of the walk: 7 miles. OS Map Landranger series No. 100 (inn GR 669975).

This is a walk of grouse butts and ling, and a trout-filled river Dove; a charming, if in places strenuous, ambit of western Farndale.

The Walk

Turn left from the inn and follow the road, dropping down to the bridge over the river Dove. Continue uphill and turn right at the junction. Opposite the deserted Monket House, turn left on a rising track via crags to Rudland Rigg path.

Turn left, walking on for about ½ mile and then follow the access track on the left above the crags, heading for West Gill Beck. Swing in an arc to the left and make for Horn End Farm. Go through the gate and follow the track to the road. Turn right to Low Mill, and by a parking area turn left, following a footpath signposted 'Public Path To High Mill'. Continue along the river bank back to the inn.

Other local attractions: Hutton-le-Hole (museum and craft shops).

Bishop Monkton
The Lamb and Flag

Roadside streams lullaby the village of Bishop Monkton near Ripon and the local inn catches the mood, offering a relaxed and friendly atmosphere hardly changed in a hundred years. With a name honouring knights returning from the Holy Crusades, this one-time coaching inn has resisted the pressures to modernise, preserving its best bar in front parlour style.

Decorated with brass and fresh flowers, its walls hung with watercolours by a Yorkshire artist, this bar serves homely dishes, freshly cooked in country mode. Roast beef and gravy dip sandwiches, game pie and Yorkshire puddings are all featured as daily specials alongside grilled steaks and gammon, chicken, ham and mushroom pie, ploughman's lunch and various salads. Two well known hand-pulled Yorkshire bitter beers, Tetley and Theakston, are joined by a welcome newcomer to the Lamb and Flag – the locally brewed Hambleton Bitter, a hoppy ale which is well worth the acquaintance. Gillespie stout, Carling Black Label and Carlsberg Export lagers, and Strongbow and Woodpecker ciders add to the extensive choice. Children are welcomed for meals and a well patronised, generously appointed pool and darts room is available. A seating area to the front of the inn is particularly inviting.

The inn is open from Monday to Saturday 12 noon to 3 pm and 5.30 pm to 11 pm and Sunday 12 noon to 3 pm and 7 pm to 10.30 pm.

Telephone: 0765 677322.

How to get there: The inn is in the village of Bishop Monkton near Ripon.

Parking: Park in the inn car park.

Length of the walk: 3½ miles. OS Map Landranger series No. 99 (inn GR 328664).

A quiet reach of the Ure is your companion on this leisurely country walk.

The Walk

Follow St. John's Road opposite the inn to a track opposite the Masons Arms and turn left. Walk on and, ignoring the fork to the right, proceed, dropping down 100 yards to a left turn. Continue on an overgrown path between copse and field boundaries to a stile. Cross and walk to a second stile, bearing left to the road. Turn left to a point 200 yards past the 'Bishop Monkton' sign, looking out for the entrance

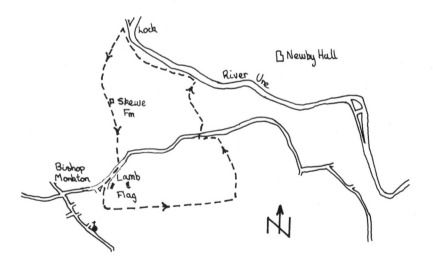

The Lamb and Flag Inn as it was in the 1920s.

to Anchor House. Turn right into the drive and turn right again following the footpath sign and the stream bank to the river.

Turn left upstream (Newby Hall is just visible above the trees on the far bank) to the Ripon Canal cut. One hundred yards before the lock gate turn left to a stile and proceed by a hedge line to a second stile, continuing on a field path to a third stile. Turn right heading for Skewe Farm buildings. Go through a gate onto a track leading back into Bishop Monkton. Turn right to the Lamb and Flag.

Other local attractions: Newby Hall and gardens.

Askrigg
The King's Arms

Fans of the BBC series 'All Creatures Great and Small' will recognise the back parlour of this delightful village inn. A set for 'The Drovers Arms', the bar surpasses its TV image in offering the most English of surroundings without theatrical contrivance, the only acknowledgement of fame being a discreet collection of photographs. Once a tack room, now sporting a stag's head, a glass-cased eel and hunting prints, the bar preserves its huge inglenook fireplace and saddle hooks impaling a wonderful collection of trophies – harnesses, clogs, flagons, old machinery and a bra and pant set. Two adjoining bars, one panelled and decorated with tapestries, are equally attractive.

Converted in the 19th century, the King's Arms was first distinguished by the artist Turner who used the inn as a base. Today it offers nine bedrooms and award winning food. Indulge in the baked Paris mushrooms with garlic butter, grilled green-lipped mussels, sauteed gambas, grilled fillet of grey mullet, whole Dover sole or beef stroganoff. Or will you settle for standard fare such as lamb cutlets or chicken, ham and mushroom pie? If you decide on a restaurant meal, it could well include sauteed galette of foie gras with brioche croutons, edged by a Madeira sauce with caramelised orange fillets, brill layered with a mousseline of salmon alongside a shellfish and pink champagne sauce, roast maize-fed guinea fowl with redcurrants and lime, and sticky toffee pudding with butterscotch sauce. Casked ale is William Younger No. 3, Tetley Bitter and McEwan 80/-. Draught Guinness, McEwan lager, Dry Blackthorn and Scrumpy Jack ciders and Becks lager are also available.

Children are welcome in the family/grill room and the inn is open from Monday to Friday 11 am to 3 pm and 7 pm to 11 pm; Saturday from 11 am to 5 pm and 7 pm to 11 pm; and Sunday from 11 am to 3 pm and 7 pm to 10.30 pm.

Telephone 0969 50258.

How to get there: The King's Arms is in the market town of Askrigg in Wensleydale.

Parking: Park on street.

Length of the walk: 3 miles. OS Map Outdoor Leisure series No. 30 (inn GR 948911).

When all is clamour at the nearby 'honeypot' of Aysgarth Falls, take this short ramble to the infinitely more spectacular Mill Gill Force, with only the thrash of the water for company. Some climbing is necessary.

81

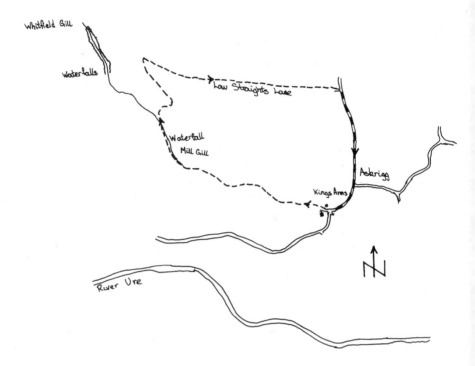

The Walk

Turn right from the inn and right again by St. Oswald's church, following the footpath sign to 'Mill Gill Force'. Take the footpath on the right near Mill Gill House across a field and continue through a gated wall to the gill. Turn right upstream and go left over a bridge, bearing right into the edge of a wood. Proceed on the footpath to a fork, deviating from your route by steering right to Mill Gill Force itself.

Go back to the fork and turn right continuing to a signpost marked 'Askrigg Via Low Straights' dropping down to the gill, then bearing right and left uphill. There are tremendous views of the leaping Whitfield Gill Force to the left. Walk on to join the well defined track known as Low Straights and turn right, noticing the looming anvil-shaped mountain of Addlebrough to your right. Continue to the road and turn right back into Askrigg.

Other local attractions: Church of St. Oswald and local woodturner's shop.

82

26 **Stainforth**
The Craven Heifer

Its name remembering a prodigious cow, the Craven Heifer sits high above a beck in the village of Stainforth. A base camp for outings to Yorkshire's famous Three Peaks, the inn offers attractive accommodation (five bedrooms), good food and prize winning ale.

The comfortable lounge bar and the dining room, both lit by colourful stained glass windows, serve homely, moderately priced bar meals ranging from traditional steak and kidney pie, steaks and Yorkshire puddings, to deep pan pizzas. For walking parties booking ahead, meat and potato pie, mixed grills and various roasts are available. Having a tradition for Yorkshire farmhouse teas going back 200 years, the inn also serves fresh baked scones and teacakes. The back room Vault Bar is reserved 'for t'lads'. Children are welcome. On fine days, the terrace overlooking the beck is the place to savour the hand-pulled Thwaites Bitter and Mild (CAMRA Pub Of The Season Award 1989). Draught Guinness, Carling Black Label and Carlsberg lagers and Strongbow cider are the alternative brews.

The inn is open from Monday to Saturday 11.30 am to 3 pm (closed Monday lunchtime in winter) and 6.30 pm (7 pm in winter) to 11 pm. Sunday hours are from 12 noon to 3 pm and 7 pm to 10.30 pm.

Telephone: 0729 822599.

How to get there: The inn is in the village of Stainforth on the B6479 north of Settle.

Parking: Park in the car park opposite the inn.

Length of the walk: 4 miles. OS Map Landranger series No. 98 (inn GR 822673).

A pleasant amble by a river seldom regarded as sporting the white rose of Yorkshire. Watch out for Lancastrian salmon (they taste no different from normal fish) and examine the kilns in the crags nearby.

The Walk

Turn left from the inn, cross the bridge and turn left again to the B6479. Cross the road and turn right and left following a sign marked 'No access to caravan site'. Descend to the river Ribble and cross by an elegant packhorse bridge. Turn left, following the river downstream on a route signposted to 'Stackhouse'. Enjoy the spectacular Stainforth Force and proceed over a series of ladder stiles for 1½ miles, passing a mill to a weir.

Cross over to the left bank via a footbridge and bear left uphill to the road, crossing and turning right over a wooden footbridge spanning the railway. Turn left along a footpath signposted 'Pike Lane'

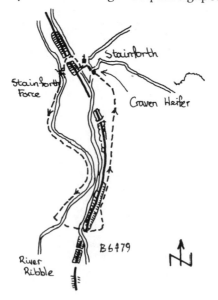

and after 200 yards turn right, following a wall uphill to a footpath signposted to Stainforth. Turn left through meadows, cross the quarry access road and climb alongside the railway track to the quarry yard. Turn left to remaining sepulchres of the once vibrant limestone industry. Turn left over a footbridge and wall, ascending past an old ruin and bearing left to the road. Turn right into Stainforth.

Other local attractions: The busy town of Settle and Victoria Cave on the moor top.

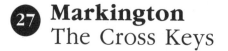

Markington
The Cross Keys

Retiring and unobtrusive on Markington's main street, the Cross Keys is a fine base for walking excursions to Fountains Abbey and Studley Park. Very much a local inn, catering for an obviously youthful village, its front rooms are primarily devoted to the joys of the cue, to the rear is a comfortably furnished lounge.

Bar snacks are simple and freshly made, offering a range of steak and gammon dishes, Yorkshire puddings with a variety of fillings, jacket potatoes, curries and sandwiches. Children are welcome. Meals are complemented by Tetley hand-pulled bitter beer, draught Guinness, Lowenbrau and Castlemaine lagers and Gaymers Olde English cider. In fine weather, the sun-trap patio and children's play area overlooking fields at the back of the inn are popular attractions.

The inn is open from Monday to Saturday from 12 noon to 3 pm (summer only) and 7 pm to 11 pm. Sunday hours are from 12 noon to 3 pm and 7 pm to 10.30 pm.

Telephone: 0765 677555.

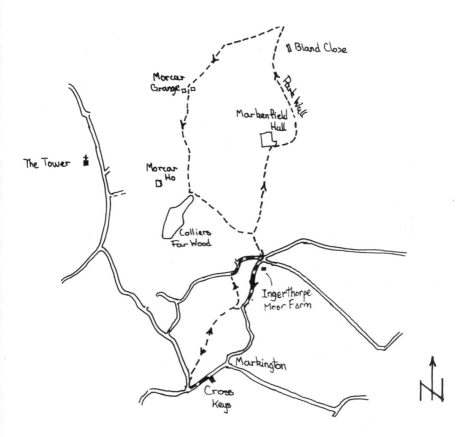

How to get there: The inn is in the village of Markington near Harrogate.

Parking: Park on the street or in the rear inn car park.

Length of the walk: 6 miles. OS Map Landranger series No. 99 (inn GR 289651).

Over ancient tracks and pathways, overgrown in places, this more demanding ramble leads to the moated, fortified manor house of Markenfield Hall. Built in 1310, this little known architectural gem is open to the public between 1st April and 31st October on Mondays only – small admission fee.

The Walk

Turn left from the inn, passing the 'Yorkshire Hussars'. Turn right on the Fountains Abbey road, crossing the little bridge and bearing right to a footpath leading to playing fields. Bearing left, cross to the field corner and follow the hedge-side down to a kissing gate. Bear right to buildings on a road bend and turn left uphill along the marked footpath (which may be overgrown) between a barn and a cottage. Continue though woodland to join a narrow road and turn right, swinging right downhill to a junction. Turn left and immediately left again along a marked public bridleway to a gate and stile. Walk on across a meadow heading for the distant battlements of Markenfield Hall, proceeding through two gates to the Hall gateway.

Turn right along an access road, dropping down and bearing left over grassland to the corner of the field and a gate. Turn left, following the footpath line of the medieval 'Park Wall', going through two more gates to join the access to Bland Close farmhouse. Turn left and go left again on a descending track skirting the edge of woodland, eventually rising to Morcar Grange Farm. Turn left through the farmyard and swing right in an arc uphill to a gate. Take the footpath across a field to a stile. Follow the field-side onwards (Morcar House Farm is to your right) to a gate and continue, guided by a barbed wire fence line down to yet another gate. Continue along a hedge to the edge of a wood and bear left on a naturally barbed track. Turn right along the bridleway you came up on and turn second right along the road to Ingerthorpe Moor Farm. Return along the footpath to Markington.

Other local attractions: Fountains Abbey and Studley Park.

Rosedale Abbey
The Milburn Arms

The high gabled Milburn Arms was originally the bailiff's and steward's house for the nearby abbey of Rosedale. A 16th century building of stone, handsomely extended in recent years to provide a colourful dining room, the inn, in a matchless landscape, offers the best in British-inspired cooking.

Changed daily, bistro style meals are served every lunchtime and evening in the low-beamed bar, offering a wide and unusual choice. Prize-winning rabbit pie and game pie are firm local favourites, and fresh Whitby fish (plaice, halibut, haddock, cod and salmon) is often available. Pork and cider casserole, chicken forrester, duck legs in blackcurrant sauce, and variously filled granary buns are also popular. To finish, sorbets, sticky toffee pudding and steamed treacle pudding get top marks. Children are welcome. Guests in the eleven bedroomed inn usually dine in the Priory Restaurant, where a typical menu includes honeydew melon and strawberries in strawberry wine, cream of cauliflower soup, lamb best end with a herb crust, fillet of turbot, steamed breast of chicken wrapped in Chinese leaves, ragout of game in puff pastry, and fillet of beef with a red wine sauce. The bar serves

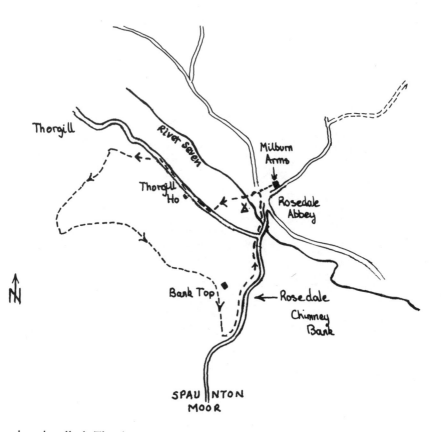

hand-pulled Theakston Bitter, Old Peculier, and Younger No. 3, together with draught Guinness, Becks and Carlsberg lagers and an impressive selection of wines. The inn has a witching post, a comfortable residents lounge with period features, a library and a shady beer garden.

Opening hours are from Monday to Saturday 11.30 am to 3 pm and 6.30 pm to 11 pm and Sunday from 12 noon to 3 pm and 7 pm to 10.30 pm.

Telephone: 075 15 312.

How to get there: The inn is in the village of Rosedale Abbey, 7 miles north of the A170 Thirsk to Scarborough road.

Parking: Park in the car park adjacent to the inn.

Length of the walk: 5 miles. OS Map Landranger series No. 100 (inn GR 724960).

This is a healthy climb to the moors, exploring the archaeology of Rosedale's iron-ore industry.

The Walk

Turn right from the inn, cross the road to the village green and turn right to the back of the church. Turn left on a footpath through a camping ground and cross a stream via a white footbridge. Bear left over a stile through a meadow to a quiet road and turn right passing Hob House and Thorgill House. Continue on the road and turn left along a footpath signposted 'Thorgill Only'. Leave the footpath on a road bend and turn left, ascending on a footpath signposted 'To Farndale'. Immediately past the houses numbered 8 and 9, turn left through a gate onto the moor.

Follow the path by the stream uphill, and keep to the wall through bracken to a stile. Continue to a second stile, threading through characteristic ling, bilberry and sphagnum moss. Where the fence line ends turn left heading away from the stream, following sheep tracks to a cairn. Walk away from the cairn in the direction of the moor top and turn left along the old track of the mineral railway.

Walk on to the building at Bank Top and bear left on a grassy track to the summit of Rosedale Chimney Bank (reputedly the steepest hill in England – the gradient in places is 1 in 2.5) and the remains of old furnaces. Turn left down the hill back to Rosedale Abbey.

Other local attractions: Hutton-le-Hole museum and craft shops.

Westow
The Blacksmith's Arms

Taking its name from the old village forge, whose character smoulders on in a massive hearth, the Blacksmith's Arms is a typically local inn. Catering for farmers and parties of walkers, cyclists and canoeists, the inn offers simple, no nonsense fare, served either in the main bar or in the tastefully furnished dining area.

Mostly home-made, the meals are both wholesome and moderately priced and children are welcomed. A favourite with visitors is the special recipe blacksmith's steak and kidney pie with mushrooms. Pork chops, steaks and vegetarian pinto bean provencal are also popular. Hazelnut meringue tops the list of sweets. Beer, lager and cider drinkers are well catered for, having the choice of John Smith Bitter, Magnet, Tetley Bitter, Foster's and Carlsberg Hof lagers, and Scrumpy Jack, Taunton Autumn Gold and Dry Blackthorn ciders. Guinness and Beamish Stout are also available. The Blacksmith's has a trophy filled games room (they also play boules) and a small beer garden.

Closed on Mondays, the inn is open during the rest of the week from Tuesday to Saturday 12 noon to 3 pm and 7 pm to 11 pm and Sunday 12 noon to 3 pm and 7 pm to 10.30 pm.

Telephone: 065381 365.

How to get there: The inn is in the village of Westow near Malton.

Parking: Park in the small car park at the side of the inn.

Length of the walk: 8½ miles. OS Map Landranger series No. 100 (inn GR 753653).

In communion with the peace and solitude of the Derwent valley, on this long and varied walk, with some climbing, you will find the ruins of a 12th century priory, a Jacobean Hall and river banks thick with flowers.

The Walk

Turn right from the inn and take the Kirkham road on the left. After 100 yards turn right along a footpath near the rather redundant sign 'Unsuitable For Motor Vehicles'. Continue on to the road and cross into the hamlet of Firby. Pass the Hall and turn left through a gate, keeping right by the fence side. Go through two mesh gates and cross a field to a footpath sign. Cross the next field diagonally, but if crops are growing turn left and right along field boundaries, to a footpath sign marked 'Centenary Way'. Turn right along the road and right

The ruins of 12th century Kirkham Priory.

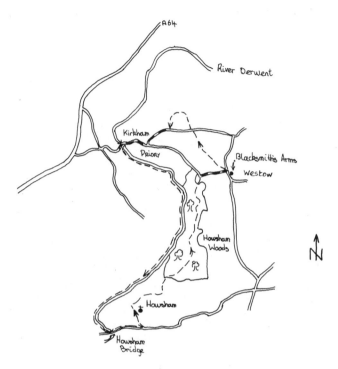

again to Kirkham Priory (in the care of English Heritage – admission fee).

Cross the bridge over the Derwent and turn left on the footpath downstream (come in July for the bi-plane regatta of dragon and damsel flies). Pass Howsham Hall on the far bank and a weir and turn left at Howsham Bridge uphill.

Turn left following the road sign 'Howsham Only' and immediately past the church, turn right along a track to a stile. Keeping to the edge of arable fields cross three further stiles and turn left down a slope between two ponds towards the south-west corner of Howsham Wood. Enter the wood and turn right on rising ground, following a footpath on the wood edge, and then gradually swinging away to the left. Turn right at a T intersection of footpaths and keep right for 1 ¼ miles to join the Westow-Kirkham road. Turn right and right again into Westow.

Other local attractions: Castle Howard and Eden Camp (a Second World War prison camp experience north of Malton).

Stutton
The Hare and Hounds

On the edge of the brooding Towton Moor, the 18th century Hare and Hounds attracts a lively trade. Very popular with customers from nearby Leeds, the inn is renowned for home-cooked food and wide choice.

Served in the attractive dining area or in the traditionally ornamented bar, blackboard specials impressively match the seasons, offering a change of menu every lunchtime and evening. Starters include cream of chicken and sweetcorn soup, avocado and prawns, and melon and raspberries. Main courses such as escalope of veal schnitzel, medallions of fillet steak stuffed with Stilton cheese, pork fillet Bearnaise and baked hake, vie for popularity alongside Moby Dick haddock and steak and mushroom pie and salad dishes. Variety continues in the faultless recitation by the landlady of an ode to 25 different sweets, listing home-made bombes, meringues, fruit pies, crumbles and tarts. A different vegetarian dish is prepared daily and children are welcome. The house ale is hand-pulled Samuel Smith Bitter from the wood alongside Ayingerbrau lager. Fresh posies, hanging flower baskets and a large rear beer garden are notable features of the Hare and Hounds.

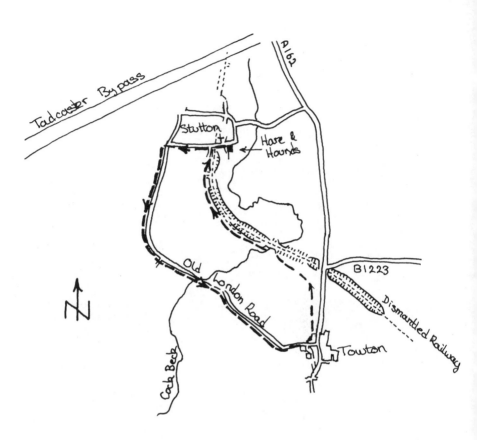

Opening times are Monday-Saturday 11.30 am-3 pm and 6.30 pm-11 pm, and Sunday 12 noon-3 pm and 7 pm-10.30 pm. Meals are served every evening except on Sundays and Mondays. Reservations are only taken for Sunday lunch.

Telephone: 0937 833164.

How to get there: The inn is in the village of Stutton near Tadcaster.

Parking: Park in the inn car park.

Length of the walk: 3 miles. OS Map Landranger series No. 105 (inn GR 481415).

A gentle stroll (at first) along the Old London Road to Towton, with a wilder return route crossing the Cock Beck.

The Walk

Turn left from the inn past the village hall and left down Malt Kiln Terrace. Turn left again up Brant Lane, ascending a makeshift track to join the Old London Road. Turn left at the back of a wood, descending between two quarries to the Cock Beck footbridge near a new golf course. Continue uphill to the back of Towton village.

Turn left at Rockingham Farm, following a hedge, ditch and white marker posts to join a field access intersecting from the right. Turn left along a hedge side to a stile and cross, keeping to the middle of a meadow, walking unerringly to a ramshackle bridge over the darkest reaches of the Cock. Bear left through a thicket and cross a stile into a field, following the track of an old railway line and bearing left past a farm bungalow to join a metalled road back to Stutton.

Other local attractions: Grimston Park Garden Centre.

③① Lockton
The Fox and Rabbit

Atop a lonely brow, near the moorland village of Lockton, this former farmhouse was converted in the 18th century to victual the Whitby stage. A boon to travellers still, it has since been extended to provide twin dining areas with extensive views, a more than adequate games and pool area, and a large bar, suitably trophied with the heads of the eponymous duo.

The only Fox and Rabbit in the country today offers the most substantial of travellers' fare. Alongside robust, hand-pulled real brews – Banks's Bitter, Cameron Bitter and Strongarm, draught Guinness and Strongbow and Woodpecker ciders (Kronenbourg and Harp lagers are also on offer) – generous home-cooked bar meals are always available at very reasonable prices. Blossoming amongst the steak dishes, juicy gammon, duckling, steak and kidney pie and lasagne, an attractive range of vegetarian dishes are increasingly popular. Children are welcome, and full dining facilities are bookable for parties. Dispensing the stirrup cup to the famous Saltersgate Hunt, the inn is the place to be on Boxing Day.

Opening times are from 12 noon to 3 pm and 7 pm to 11 pm Monday to Saturday and 12 noon to 3 pm and 7 pm to 10.30 pm on Sunday. The pub is closed Tuesdays from October to March.

Telephone: 0751 60213.

How to get there: The inn is on the A169, 6 miles north-east of Pickering.

Parking: Park in the inn car park.

Length of the walk: 5 miles. OS Map Landranger series No. 100 (inn GR 846883).

A four-dales spectacular, discovering the very best of the English countryside.

The Walk

Take the footpath at the rear of the inn, turning right to the Fox and Rabbit farm track. Enter a caravan/camping field and follow the right-hand hedge down to a stile. Cross and descend to a wood. Turn right and swing left on a descending path to the valley of the Dalby Beck. Continue over a stile along a green track to cross the beck at the entrance to High Dalby House. Turn left upstream to a white gate and the peace and tranquillity of Staindale Lodge. Walk uphill through the wood, with its profusion of wild flowers and occasional deer, to the A169. Turn left to Lockton village.

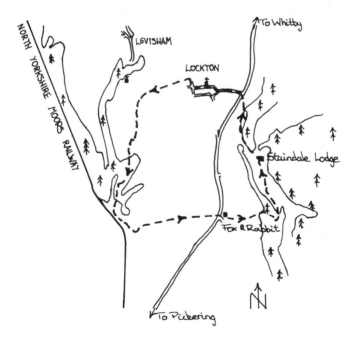

Beyond the church, turn right following a signposted path between the last two houses. Proceed along the giddy crest, then follow a zig-zag path downhill to a dog-leg in the Lockton-Levisham road and turn left on a bridlepath. The forlorn Levisham church is in the dell on your right. Follow the Levisham Beck (keeping your eyes peeled for otters) to Newton Dale, steering left by a sea of gorse to the valley of Cross Dale. Ascend steeply left and aiming left of Farfields Farm, take a walled track back to the A169 and the inn.

Other local attractions: Dalby Forest Drive (toll payable), Thorton Dale village.

32 **Grewelthorpe**
The Crown

A dapper village pub on the ancient packhorse route between Kirkby Malzeard and Masham, the busy Crown happily marries local character with facilities for the increasingly discerning diner.

Wrought iron tables furnish the compact low-beamed bar which comes complete with brasses and its own rustic ghost. A small but attractive dining area at the rear offers a varied blackboard menu featuring a selection of steak and chop dishes, pork fillet in spicy apricot sauce, lemon sole and prawns and game in season. Sweets again offer a wide choice, ranging from jam sponge and custard to a brandy snap basket filled with sorbet and fresh fruit. Hand-pulled ale is from the Theakston and Tetley stables. Draught Guinness and Bulmers cider, and Carlsberg Hof, Harp and McEwan lagers are also available. Sporting traditions add to the Crown's friendly personality, the inn fielding its own teams for football, cricket, golf and quoits, played on a specially laid out pitch adjacent to the rear car park.

The inn is open from Tuesday-Saturday 11 am to 11 pm (Monday – evening only from 7 pm) and on Sunday from 12 noon to 3 pm and 7 pm to 10.30 pm.

Telephone: 0765 658210.

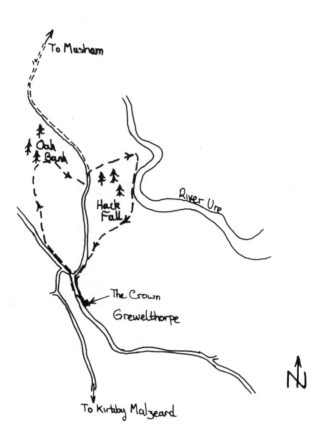

How to get there: The inn is in the village of Grewelthorpe on the minor road between Masham and Kirkby Malzeard.

Parking: Park in the inn car park.

Length of the walk: 3½ miles. OS Map Landranger series No. 99 (inn GR 231763).

An invigorating woodland walk (which can be muddy in wet weather) discovering the little known delights of Hackfall, a river gorge planted with 18th century follies as a romantic contrast to the more formal landscape at nearby Fountains Abbey.

The Walk

Heading north past the church and the Hackfall Inn, take the left hand fork to Ilton and walk uphill for 200 yards to a marked footpath on your right. Proceed diagonally across a meadow, crossing several stiles to the edge of Oak Bank Wood. Turn right through a gate and walk downhill on the edge of the wood (keep a drystone wall to your right) to join a track. Turn right to the Masham road. Bearing left, cross the road and continue over grassland downhill into Hackfall Woods.

Enter a gated entrance signposted by the Woodland Trust and bear right on a botanically exciting route to the river Ure and a golden beach! Continue on a web of climbing boggy paths on a highly compulsive search for the Rustic Temple, Fisher's Hall, and Mowbray Castle (and there are more mouldering gems). The way out is by a track, heading south-west from the octagonal, lancet-windowed Fisher's Hall. The track companions a stream uphill to Hackfall Farm and Grewelthorpe.

Other local attractions: Mock Druid Temple near Leighton Reservoir.

Cawood
The Ferry

A characterful, jolly little inn with wispy associations with Cardinal Wolsey, the 16th century Ferry Inn sits quietly by the Ouse swing bridge in the river town of Cawood. Inglenooked, oak beamed and decorated with a fascinating display of curios, the inn preserves in its marvellously unaltered nooks and crannies the intimacy so essential to treasonous plottings. The disgraced ecclesiastic himself is said to have been a customer. If only walls could tell! Scanning the inn's menu and a wall mounted board listing the ingredients for Cawood Castle's Great Feast of 1564, customers may suppose another historical connection.

The Ferry is locally famous for its dozen or so vegetarian specialities – Red Dragon Pie (a concoction of aduki beans in a herbed mushroom and tomato sauce with a Swiss style cheese topping), spicy garbanzo beans, spinach and walnut lasagne and mushroom and nut fettucini. Non vegetarians are amply catered for in a range of meat and fish dishes, notably Chinese style chicken wings, gammon steak and home-made steak and kidney pie. Meals can be enjoyed in the beer garden or on an elevated platform affording views of the river to the rear of the inn. Children are welcome. For ale drinkers with a taste for hand-pulled excellence, the Ferry offers Mansfield Riding Bitter, Old Bailey Strong, Adnams Broadside and Adnams Southwold bitters and Ridley IPA. Lager drinkers can select from Red Stripe, Castlemaine, Kaliber, Grolsch and McEwan. Murphy's Irish stout is also available, and for spirit drinkers, doubles of whisky and gin are the cheapest in the area.

Well run by a family quartet, the inn is open from 11 am to 11 pm Monday to Saturday and Sunday 12 noon to 3 pm and 7 pm to 10.30 pm. There are four letting rooms for bed and breakfast.

Telephone: 0757 268515.

How to get there: The inn is on the south bank of the Ouse, near the junction of the B1222 with the B1223 in Cawood near Selby.

Parking: Park in the inn car park or in the car park to the right of the bridge behind the floodbank.

Length of the walk: 5 miles. OS Map Landranger series No. 105 (inn GR 574378).

This 'Wolsey Walk' treads the ancient precincts of Cawood Castle, which was once the home of the ill fated Cardinal Wolsey. The route also visits the confluence of the Wharfe and the Ouse and the Norman church of All Saints.

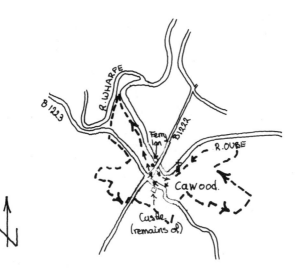

The Walk

Leaving the inn, walk downstream along Old Road and turn right to the junction with Thorpe Lane. Turn right again, passing the splendid remains of Cawood Castle. Continue to the traffic lights and turn right and left past the Ferry Inn. Continue on a well marked path by the riverside, crossing four footbridges and two stiles to view Wharfe's Mouth, and return along the footpath, turning right by a large tree to the banks of the Wharfe. Follow the cart track to the road, turn left and right by the Northingales Fish Pond sign and follow footpath signs around field edges to the B1222 and the Bay Horse Inn.

Turn left to the second bridge on the right and turn right along a footpath alongside Castle Garth (home of the greater crested newt), merging with a tarmac path. Cross a stile and a road, bear left, cross another two stiles and turn left to Wistowgate. Continue and turn right down Oxfield Lane, along three sides of a large oblong field and turn right (Ings Lane) and left to the river bank and the church of All Saints. Follow the river bank back to the inn. (A leaflet describing the walk in more detail is available from the Recreation Footpath Section, North Yorkshire County Surveyors Office, County Hall, Northallerton DL7 8AH.)

Other local attractions: All Saints church.

Cawood Castle
15th January 1564

A Great Feast to Celebrate
The Enthronement of
George Neville as The Archbishop of York

MENU

500 partridges	400 mallard and	2000 geese
400 woodcocks	teales	104 peacocks
400 plovers	2000 chickens	100 dozen quayles
608 pykes and	200 feasantes	4000 conies
breams	500 stags bucks	500 tuns of ale
12 porpoises and	and roes	100 tuns of wine
seals	300 quarters of	1000 dishes of jelly
4000 pasties of cold	wheat	4000 cold baked
venison	6 wylde bulls	tarts
304 yorkes	104 oxen	3000 cold baked
1000 capons	1000 muttons	custards
	304 neals	2000 hot. custards

34 Cray
The White Lion

This 17th century hostelry in the Yorkshire Dales National Park served its apprenticeship victualling drovers. On the tortuous road between Wharfedale and Bishopdale, the isolated White Lion nourishes pedestrian traffic still, being at the centre of some of the finest tramping country in Yorkshire.

Restored in the grand tradition, preserving beams, stone-flagged floors and log fires, the inn serves both lunchtime and evening meals either in the bar or cosy dining room. The mid-day fare, supplemented by daily specials such as steak and mushrooms in ale and barbecued pork, includes home-made steak and kidney pie, local chicken and Yorkshire pudding filled with Cumberland sausage. The night time menu offers freshly roasted topside of beef with Yorkshire pudding, onion gravy and horseradish sauce, pan fried gammon steak in oriental-style sauce and trout topped with almond butter. A children's menu is also available and dogs are welcome. The inn has a distinguished reputation for fine ales, having won the title 'Pub of the Year 1991' for the finely cellared beer known as Moorhouse's Premier Draught. Also on tap are Tetley Bitter, Moorhouse's Bitter, Pendle

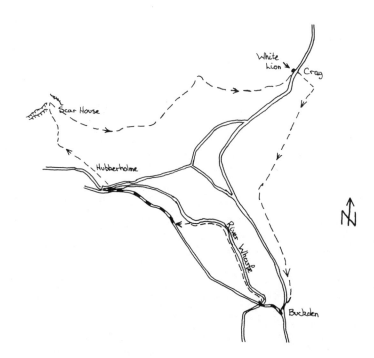

Witches Brew, Carlsberg lager and Strongbow cider. And don't forget the tea and coffee. Converted from an adjacent barn, an annexe provides five en-suite bedrooms. A magnetic attraction for children is the tinkling Cray Gill opposite the inn.

In the winter months opening times are Monday to Friday 11 am to 3 pm and 6 pm to 11 pm, Saturdays 11 am to 11 pm and Sundays 12 noon to 3 pm and 7 pm to 11 pm. In the summer months they are Monday to Saturday 10 am to 11 pm and Sundays 10 am to 3 pm and 7 pm to 11 pm.

Telephone: 0756 760262.

How to get there: The inn is in the tiny settlement of Cray on the steep road 1½ miles north of Buckden on the B6160.

Parking: Parking opposite the inn is limited and at a premium in the height of the tourist season. A large 'pay and display' car park is available at Buckden.

Length of the walk: 6 miles. OS Map Outdoor Leisure series No. 30 (inn GR 943793).

The Walk

Cross the Cray Gill, go through a gate and turn right following the footpath marked to Buckden. Climb, bearing left to the first ridge and pick up a green track. Turn right along Buckden Rake into Rakes Wood. Enjoy the spectacular views of the Wharfe valley, but beware of screes and supposedly sure-footed sheep. One clumsy beast brought down half the hillside and nearly put paid to my tramping days. Descend on the track to Buckden.

Turn right by the green along Dubbs Lane and cross the bridge, turning immediately right along the riverside footpath signposted 'Hubberholme Dales Way'. Rejoin Dubbs Lane and turn right to Hubberholme. Turn right by the George, recross the river on a bridge and turn left to the back of the church on a footpath signposted 'Scar House, Yockenthwaite and Dales Way'. Climb steeply to the melancholy Scar House and turn right on the arcing footpath at the rear of Hubberholme Wood and Todds Wood. Cross Crook Gill and walk downhill into Cray.

Other local attractions: Buckden Pike and Buckden village.

Acaster Malbis
The Ship

The 17th century Ship enjoys all the delights of the river Ouse. With private moorings and fishing rights, a nautically spruced restaurant, a conservatory and an inglenooked bar, visitors could well be shanghaied for the whole summer. A port of call for cruise parties from York and a popular haunt of holiday-makers and hikers, the inn serves excellent home-made meals and real ale.

The bar menu features double-decker sandwiches, breaded mushrooms with garlic mayonnaise, salmon shanties (salmon morsels mixed with broccoli and cheese, coated in breadcrumbs and fried), jumbo Yorkshire puddings, chilli con carne and a whopping Yorkshire grill which includes rump steak, gammon, lamb chop, sausage, liver, kidney, black pudding and fried egg. Daily specials are available, as are children's portions. Seafood is prominent on the extensive restaurant menu. Enjoy the seafood cocktail, potted shrimps, devilled whitebait, halibut steak with prawn and caper sauce, salmon veronique or the lemon sole. Medallions of fillet beef in a port and Stilton sauce, fillet of pork with apples and sage in a cream and cider sauce, calves liver, and char-grilled steaks, are all memorable alternatives. Vegetarians are catered for in a choice of seven dishes. Tetley Bitter and Mild and Timothy Taylor Landlord hand-pulled beers are well presented alongside draught Guinness, Lowenbrau, Castlemaine, Skol and Carlsberg lagers and Gaymers Olde English cider. The Ship has a notable wine cellar and eight en-suite bedrooms.

Opening times are from Monday to Saturday 11 am to 3 pm and 6.30 pm to 11 pm and Sunday 12 noon to 3 pm and 7 pm to 10.30 pm.

Telephone: 0904 705609.

How to get there: The inn is on the right bank of the Ouse, in the village of Acaster Malbis, downstream of York.

Parking: Landlubbers can park in the inn car park – aquatics may use the private moorings (but obtain permission first).

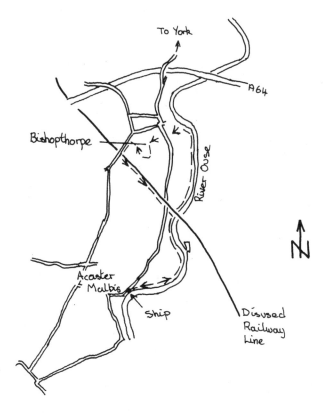

Length of the walk: 4½ miles. OS Map Landranger series No. 105 (inn GR 590456).

This fascinating riverside walk offers an inspection tour of river craft (spot the most outlandish names), with the added temptation of a stowaway afternoon in York.

The Walk
Turn left from the inn along the road to Bishopthorpe and after 200 yards take the right-hand track passing by a caravan park. Continue under a defunct railway bridge (the British Transport Yacht Club compound is under the span) to the Bishop's Restaurant and a slipway. There is an opportunity here for lazy swabs to take the return river bus into York, sailing every day Easter to October at 10 am and 11.30 am and 1 pm, 2.30 pm and 4 pm, telephone 0904 704442/705812.

Proceed along Ferry Lane and cross a road into a housing estate, walking down Montague Road. Swing left and turn right along Maple Avenue past Bishopthorpe Health Centre to the Acaster Malbis road and turn left. Cross the bridge and turn right, right and right again to join a footpath (under the bridge you've just crossed) along an old railway line. Walk down the track to the previously encountered bridge over the river and scramble down the bank, back to the riverside path next to the British Transport Yacht Club compound. Turn right to Acaster Malbis.

Other local attractions: The myriad pleasures of York.

112

36 Ramsgill
The Yorke Arms

The ivy clad Yorke Arms breathes repose, a quiet transition from the roisterous days of tally-ho when the building was first erected by the eponymous Yorke family for use as a hunting lodge. Rebuilt as an inn in 1843, the structure retains many fine features, enhanced internally by a variety of antiques and by a particularly eye-catching collection of period pewter. Inspired by the Yorke family motto emblazoned on the inn sign ('with God's help I can scale any wall') a substantial refurbishment of the inn has recently been carried out to provide 13 en-suite bedrooms, a residents' lounge and an elegantly furnished restaurant dominated by an enormous looking-glass and an heirloom server, combining to create a relaxing atmosphere.

The theme is echoed in traditional wholesome menus and a comprehensive wine list. Appetisers range from potted Stilton with port and prawn cocktail topped with caviar, to asparagus spears on toast topped with a cheese sauce. Fish and main courses are equally varied and include white fish Creole, sauteed Nidderdale trout stuffed with prawns, smoked salmon and herring roes, and duckling with a brandy and orange sauce. A range of speciality ice-cream platters strike the grand finale. Bar meals again are of good quality offering such local delicacies as black-pudding thermidor, Nidderdale lamb chops and

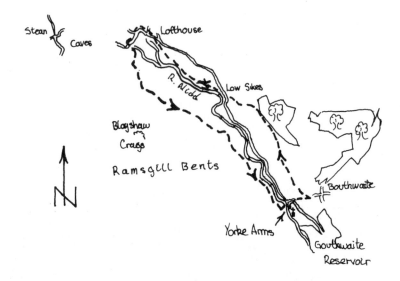

delicacies as black-pudding thermidor, Nidderdale lamb chops and trout with almonds and grapes. Facilities for the dedicated ale connoisseur are rather limited at the Yorke Arms, but a fine snug, furnished with settles and surveyed by interesting carved corbels, serves Younger Scotch Bitter, McEwan lager, Becks lager and Blackthorn Dry cider.

For non resident diners, the inn is open for bar lunches 12 noon-1.45 pm every day, for restaurant lunches from Tuesday to Saturday (reservations only) 12 noon to 1.30 pm and Sunday 12 noon to 1.45 pm; and for dinner from Tuesday to Saturday from 7.30 pm to 9 pm and Sunday 7.30 pm to 8.30 pm. Licensing hours are from 11 am to 11 pm every day apart from Sunday, 12 noon to 3 pm and 7 pm to 10.30 pm.

Telephone: 0423 755243.

How to get there: The inn is in the village of Ramsgill on a minor road skimming Gouthwaite Reservoir, 4½ miles from Pateley Bridge.

Parking: Park by the village green.

Length of the walk: 4½ miles. OS Map Landranger series No. 99 (inn GR 118711).

A gentle ramble through peaceful fields along the beautiful Nidd valley.

114

The Walk

Leaving the inn, turn right along the road to the arched bridge over the Nidd and turn right again along a lane signposted to Bouthwaite. Pass the Methodist church and turn left following the well marked Nidderdale Way. Crossing Lul Beck, bear right over a stile and climb to Low Longside House. Taking a right fork, continue to the rear of Longside House. With the wood to your right, walk on and take a diagonally descending footpath towards Low Sikes Farm to join the track of the old Nidderdale Light Railway. This was built in the 1900s to haul men and materials to the dam construction site in the high dale. The navvies were rather partial to inns themselves and tales of the Saturday sessions are colourful in the extreme.

Cross the road by an iron bridge over the Nidd. Follow the footpath sign through fields for a further mile and rejoin the road. Turn left into the village of Lofthouse and left again, crossing the bridge at How Stean. Turn left once more (on the left bank of the beck an old limekiln is preserved) and by a caravan park turn right up a steep hill to a signpost. Turn right along a route that cannot be lost (if you can avoid stumbling over rabbits) back to Ramsgill.

Other local attractions: How Stean Gorge (Little Switzerland) and Gouthwaite Reservoir (a nature reserve attracting many species of birds, including the golden eagle).

Thixendale
The Cross Keys

In this peaceful valley of 16 dales, the Cross Keys is the home of the legendary quiet pint. Very much a village pub involved with the local community, it is simple, cosy and unpretentious, looking out on a hill grazed by pedigree goats.

Decorated with village photographs and commendations (notably a certificate of merit in the Ryedale Ploughman's Lunch of the Year Award 1987), its L-shaped bar offers suitably home-made refreshments according to the season – braised pheasant, hare in stout and rabbit casserole, together with pasties, ham and eggs and steak and Guinness pie, and the intriguing 'painslack handful', a very special buttie served in granary bread, whose recipe is a closely guarded secret. Children over 14 only are welcomed for meals, although the pub has a pleasant beer garden to the rear for youngsters. Hand-pulled Tetley Bitter, Jennings Bitter, Strongow cider and two lagers, Carlsberg Pilsner and Hof, are available. Family run, the Cross Keys, and the adjacent tea-rooms are popular refuelling stops along the Wolds Way.

Between 1st November and Easter Monday, the pub is closed on Monday lunchtimes. Opening times apart from this, are Monday to Saturday 12 noon to 3 pm and 6 pm to 11 pm, and Sunday 12 noon to 3 pm and 7 pm to 10.30 pm.

Telephone: 0377 88272.

How to get there: The inn is in the village of Thixendale, off the A166 York to Driffield road.

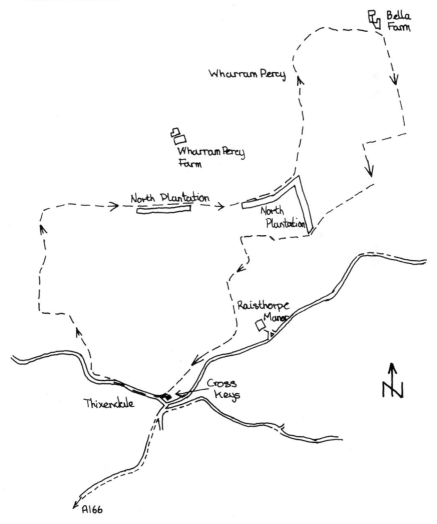

Parking: Park on the road fronting the inn, or in Thixendale village.

Length of the walk: 8 miles. OS Map Landranger series No. 100 (inn GR 845611).

A long and pleasant undulating walk, tramping the feather-bed contours of the wolds and visiting the medieval village of Wharram Percy.

The Walk

Turn left from the inn and right along Thixendale's only street (the folk hereabouts are famous for their splendid scarecrows). Turn right opposite Cottage Farm up the steep bank on the Wolds Way. Veer left by an old barn over a stile and continue fieldside to the corner. Turn left on a waymarked path fieldside and turn right at the corner downhill. Go through a gap in the hedge on your left to a stile, and ascend with the fence line to your right. Cross a stile and continue to a clump of trees and a meeting of tracks. Turn to the right along a track at the edge of North Plantation, and swing left to the site of Wharram Percy village.

Near the pond go downhill to a stile and cross to the old church, continuing uphill left onto a track leading to a disused railway bridge. Continue uphill to join the road near Bella Farm. Turn right along the road (Wold Way) and at the sharp bend continue on a track skirting the edge of a plantation. Walk on for 200 yards and turn left on a waymarked path hedgeside to the next field and immediately turn right along the field boundary, continuing on a track passing the edge of a plantation. Turn right through a bridlegate and walk on to the right of a depression towards the end of a hedge. Turn left along a track downhill following a hedge to a small gate and bear left, dropping down into a valley through a gate. Parallel to the road, continue into Thixendale and back to the inn.

Other local attractions: Wharram Percy medieval village.

Nunnington
The Royal Oak

As quiet as a mouse, the river Rye slips by the peaceful village of Nunnington, whose inn can be found on a hillside near the 13th century church of All Saints and St. James. A one time meeting place for Ryedale cobblers, the Royal Oak has been radically altered in recent years, the ruggedness of its exposed beams and stonework providing the ideal backdrop for displays of farming bygones, old bottles, jugs and flagons and a fascinating collection of keys.

Served in the twin bars, substantial home-made meals are inspired by cottage kitchen fare, using fresh local ingredients such as Wensleydale cheese, hams and country herbs. To begin the meal, spicy mushrooms, pates and a seafood cocktail of mackerel, herring and prawns are available. Both hot and cold main courses offer equal choice, the latter including open prawn boats and chicken coronation salad. Hot specialities of the house are steak and kidney casserole with herb dumplings, sea food crumble, creamy kidneys, breast of chicken in orange and tarragon sauce and lemon sole stuffed with crabmeat, together with a full range of steak and poultry dishes. The snow queen, a concoction of crushed meringue, brandy and raspberries

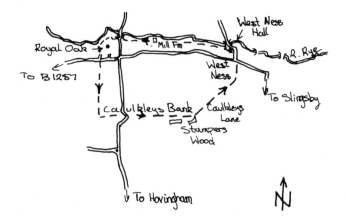

heads the retinue of sweets. Hand-pulled beers, both the bitter and the Old Peculier, are from the Theakston brewery. Bulmers Original cider and Carlsberg Export lager are also on tap. Children are welcome for meals and the inn has a small 'al fresco' area to the rear.

Opening times are Monday from 6.30 pm to 10.30 pm (closed for lunch except on Bank Holidays), Tuesday to Saturday 11.45 am to 2.30 pm and 6.30 pm to 10.30 pm (Friday and Saturday 11 pm) and Sunday 12 noon to 2 pm and 7 pm to 10.30 pm.

Telephone: 043 95271.

How to get there: The inn is in the village of Nunnington on the south bank of the Rye.

Parking: Park in the inn car park.

Length of the walk: 5½ miles. OS Map Landranger series No. 100 (inn GR 666793).

A ramble of high vistas, enjoying the tranquillity of Ryedale with several opportunities for pool-watching along the Rye.

The Walk

Turn right from the inn uphill past the church, crossing the road without deviation to join a track. Proceed for ¾ mile to a line of dead trees and turn left, crossing the road and continuing along Caulkleys Bank. Turn left down Caulkleys Lane (a hedged track) to join the road. Turn left and first right on the road signposted 'Welham and

120

Kirkbymoorside' to a sign marked 'West Ness', and bear left to the bridge.

Turn left upstream past Mill Farm (notice the old mill-wheel and mill race) to the weir and approach the back of Nunnington Hall, heading left to a gate. Proceed past a double gabled house and turn right over a stile into what appears to be a private garden. Turn left along a gravelled drive, turn right, and turn left again before the bridge, back to the inn.

Other local attractions: Nunnington Hall (a National Trust property displaying an interesting collection of dolls' houses).

Pickering
The White Swan

An old coaching inn, the White Swan has been sensitively modernised, preserving much of its colourful past. With small twin bars, furnished with black-lead hearths, the inn offers a bar menu of freshness and versatility. Try the smoked Pickering trout, char-grilled Barnsley chop, braised chicken in chasseur sauce, a French ploughman's lunch or a round of sandwiches. More formal meals are served in the attractive St. Emilion Room. The Ogen melon laced with port and marooned in crushed ice is an ideal aperitif. Other starters include French snails in jacket potatoes glazed with garlic butter, and choux buns stuffed with crab meat. Main courses range from escalope of wild boar, pan fried quail, and fillet of salmon and monkfish simmered in St. Emilion and encased in puff pastry, to roast rack of English lamb and pork fillet with artichokes. The White Swan has a reputation for fine wines, and hand-pulled Theakston and Cameron Bitters, draught Guinness, Carlsberg Hof lager and Strongarm cider attract a discerning trade. The inn has 13 en-suite bedrooms with full facilities, and a very comfortable private lounge. Both children and dogs are welcome.

Licensing hours are Monday from 11 am to 11 pm, Tuesday to Saturday 11 am to 3 pm and 6 pm to 11 pm, and Sunday 12 noon to 3 pm and 7 pm to 10.30 pm.
Telephone: 0751 72288.

How to get there: The inn is in the Market Place, Pickering.

Parking: Park in the inn car park.

Length of the walk: 6 miles. OS Map Landranger series No. 100 (inn GR 797841).

A sylvan adventure, offering leafy glades and encounters with steam trains and trout-filled pools.

The Walk

Leaving the inn, turn left up Burgate and turn first right past the allotments to Hatcase Lane and the A169. Turn left and fork left on a footpath by 'Aysgarth', cutting through a new housing estate to open fields. Follow the footpath alongside Lowther and Little Park Woods for 1½ miles to a gate on the left. Go through. Immediately right over a wall, take a descending woodland path to Pickering Beck. Take great care and watch out for steam trains chugging along the North Yorkshire Moors Railway line, which you should cross.

Turn left through woods and eventually recross the line and the beck. Turn right, crossing the meadow on a left-hand track to a stile. Climb and proceed by a woodland path and estate track to merge with the road. Continue along the road. The Moorland Trout Farm is on your right. Turn left up Market Street to the inn.

Other local attractions: Pickering Castle, Beck Isle Museum, North Yorkshire Moors Steam Railway, church of St. Peter and St. Paul (important wall paintings).

40 Lofthouse
The Crown

At the head of Nidderdale, Lofthouse once had pretensions beyond its rustic station. A dam-makers railway brought the promise of a branch line and the village inn was extended to cater for the sophistication that never came. Today, the high-gabled Crown sits quietly above the picturesque Nidd gorge, offering bed and breakfast accommodation (five rooms) as a base for exploring some of the wildest scenery in Yorkshire.

The Crown has two simply furnished public rooms, both log-flamed in winter. Decoration is from the eclectic school – sobre country prints vainly fighting for attention alongside a splendid model of a steam engine made from watch and clock parts and a drawing of a device called 'The Patented Pink Pot' boasting a 'burp silencer mouthpiece', 'non-skid lip grip' and 'sobriety indicator'.

The wholesome bar menu consists of freshly made sandwiches, steak and onion baps, gammon and eggs, beef in beer (with celery, carrots, onions and herbs), rump steak and various salads. Children are welcome for meals. The house beverages are Theakston and Tetley bitters and Tetley mild, Carlsberg lager, Gaymers Olde English cider

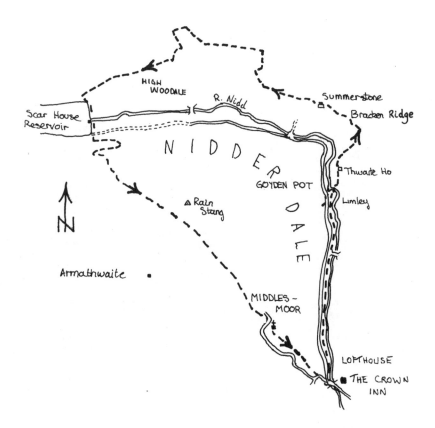

and draught Guinness. The inn has a pleasant beer garden/patio and an incredibly antiquated outside gents toilet (urgent need for Grade I listing here!).

Opening times are Monday to Saturday 12 noon to 3 pm and 7 pm to 11 pm. Sunday hours are 12 noon to 3 pm and 7 pm to 10.30 pm. Telephone: 0423 755206.

How to get there: The Crown is nearly at the end of the public highway, some 8 miles north of Pateley Bridge. Turn right just before How Steam and the Yorkshire Water access road.

Parking: Park above the inn in the signposted car park.

Length of the walk: 9 miles. Map: OS Landranger series No. 99 (inn GR 102734).

126

A more difficult walk than many others in this book, across the wild moors in a spirited hike to the Nidd's source.

The Walk

Turn left from the inn downhill to the road and turn right for 200 yards, crossing the Nidd bridge to the Yokshire Water Scar House Reservoir access road. Turn right along the access road (little traffic) for 1 ½ miles to Limley Farm and turn right. Continue left through the farmyard. At this point, the enfeebled river skulks underground into the labyrinth of Goyden Pot.

Cross the dry river bed and zig-zag up the hillside to Thwaite House. Continue on the well defined footpath, enjoying vistas of impressive Scar House dam and the looming Little Whernside beyond, passing Bracken Ridge and Summerstones Lodge. Walk on for a further ½ mile and fork right away from the dam, ascending via a dog-leg track to the moor. After a ¼ mile climb turn left onto North Moor and descend Woo Gill, passing to the top of the wood near High Woodale on a descending track to the dam top. Notice below the dam the substantial remains of a town built to house the dam construction workers in the early 1900s.

Cross the dam and turn left and sharp right, following the rising track to the summit and continue over grouse and golden plover moors for a further 2 miles to the hilltop village of Middlesmoor. Descend to the village church of St Chad and take the marked footpath through a farmyard to the Yorkshire Water access road. Turn right along the access to the road and turn left and left again back to the in.

Other local attractions: How Stean Gorge (Little Switzerland).